Daily Prayers

for

Orthodox

Christians

www.john-that-theologian.com

Publisher's Cataloguing-in-Publication data

Hutchison-Hall, John (Ellsworth).
  Daily Prayers for Orthodox Christians : A prayer book following the Tradition of the Russian Orthodox Church.
  p. cm.
    ISBN-13: 978-0615666204
    ISBN-10: 0615666205
1. Eastern Orthodox Church—Prayer books and devotions—English.
I. Hutchison-Hall, John (Ellsworth). II john-that-theologian.com. III. Title.

Library of Congress Control Number: 2012912655
BX360.A5.H8 2012
242.8019—dc22

Table of Contents

"A theologian is one who prays,
and one who prays is a theologian."

— *Evagrius of Pontus*

MORNING PRAYERS

The Prayer of St. Ephrem the Syrian

(This prayer is read on all days of Holy Great Lent, except on Saturdays and Sundays.)

O Lord and Master of my life, a spirit of idleness, despondency, ambition, and idle talking give me not. *(Prostration.)*

But rather a spirit of chastity, humble-mindedness, patience, and love bestow upon me, Thy servant. *(Prostration.)*

Yea, O Lord King, grant me to see my failings and not condemn my brother; for blessed art Thou unto the ages of ages. AMEN. *(Prostration.)*

O God, cleanse me, a sinner. *(12 times, with a reverence each time, and then the entire prayer :)*

O Lord and Master of my life, a spirit of idleness, despondency, ambition, and idle talking give me not. But rather a spirit of chastity, humble-mindedness, patience, and love bestow upon me, Thy servant. Yea, O Lord King, grant me to see my failings and not condemn my brother; for blessed art Thou unto the ages of ages. AMEN. *(Prostration.)*

*Having risen from sleep, before any other action, stand
reverently, considering thyself to be in the presence of the
All-seeing God, and, having made the sign of the Cross, say:*

IN the name of the Father, and of the Son, and of
the Holy Spirit. AMEN.

*Then pause a moment, until all thy senses are calmed and
thy thoughts forsake all things earthly: and then
make three bows, saying:*

The Prayer of the Publican

O GOD, be merciful to me, a sinner. *(Thrice)*

The Beginning Prayer

O LORD Jesus Christ, Son of God, through the
prayers of Thy most pure Mother and all the saints, have
mercy on us. AMEN.

GLORY to Thee, our God, glory to Thee.

O HEAVENLY King, The Comforter, the Spirit of
Truth, Who art everywhere present and fillest all
things, Treasury of blessings and Giver of life: Come and
abide in us, and cleanse us of every impurity, and save our
souls, O Good One.

Holy God, Holy Mighty, Holy Immortal, have
mercy on us. *(Thrice)*

Glory to the Father, and to the Son, and to the
Holy Spirit, both now and ever, and unto the ages
of ages. AMEN.

O Most Holy Trinity, have mercy on us.

O Lord, blot out our sins.

O Master, pardon our iniquities.

O Holy One, visit and heal our infirmities for Thy name's sake.

Lord, have mercy. *(Thrice)*

Glory to the Father, and to the Son, and to the Holy Spirit, both now and ever, and unto the ages of ages. AMEN.

OUR FATHER, Who art in heaven, hallowed be Thy name. Thy kingdom come, Thy will be done, on earth as it is in heaven. Give us this day our daily bread, and forgive us our debts, as we forgive our debtors; and lead us not into temptation, but deliver us from the evil one.

Troparia to the Holy Trinity

HAVING risen from sleep, we fall down before Thee, O Good One, and the angelic hymn we cry aloud to Thee, O Mighty One. Holy, Holy, Holy art Thou, O God, through the Theotokos, have mercy on us.

Glory to the Father, and to the Son, and to the Holy Spirit.

From bed and sleep Thou hast raised me up, O Lord: enlighten my mind and heart and open my lips that I may hymn Thee, O Holy Trinity:

Holy, Holy, Holy art Thou, O God, through the Theotokos, have mercy on us.

Both now and ever, and unto the ages of ages. AMEN.

Suddenly the judge shall come, and the deeds of each shall be laid bare; but with fear do we cry at midnight. Holy, Holy, Holy art Thou, O God, through the Theotokos, have mercy on us.

Lord, have mercy. *(Twelve times)*

Prayer of Saint Basil the Great to the Most Holy Trinity

AS I rise from sleep I thank Thee, O Holy Trinity, for through Thy great goodness and patience Thou wast not angered with me, an idler and sinner, nor hast Thou destroyed me in my sins, but hast shown Thy usual love for mankind, and when I was prostrate in despair, Thou hast raised me to keep the morning watch and glorify Thy power. And now enlighten my mind's eye and open my mouth to study Thy words and understand Thy commandments and do Thy will, and hymn Thee in heartfelt adoration and praise Thy Most Holy Name of the Father, and of the Son, and of the Holy Spirit, both now and ever, and unto the ages of ages. AMEN.

O come let us worship God our King. *(Bow)*

O come let us worship and fall down before Christ our King and God. *(Bow)*

O come let us worship and fall down before Christ Himself, our King and God. *(Bow)*

Psalm 50

HAVE mercy on me, O God, according to Thy great mercy; and according to the multitude of Thy compassions blot out my transgression. Wash me thoroughly from mine iniquity, and cleanse me from my sin.

For I know mine iniquity, and my sin is ever before me. Against Thee only have I sinned and done this evil before Thee, that Thou mightest be justified in Thy words, and prevail when Thou art judged.

For behold, I was conceived in iniquities, and in sins did my mother bear me. For behold, Thou hast loved truth; the hidden and secret things of Thy wisdom hast Thou made manifest unto me.

Thou shalt sprinkle me with hyssop, and I shall be made clean; Thou shalt wash me, and I shall be made whiter than snow.

Thou shalt make me hear joy and gladness; the bones that have been humbled will rejoice.

Turn Thy face away from my sins, and blot out all mine iniquities.

Create in me a clean heart, O God, and renew a right spirit within me.

Cast me not away from Thy presence, and take not Thy Holy Spirit from me.

Restore unto me the joy of Thy salvation, and with Thy governing Spirit establish me.

I shall teach transgressors Thy ways, and the ungodly shall turn back unto Thee.

Deliver me from blood-guiltiness. O God, Thou God of my salvation; my tongue shall rejoice in Thy righteousness.

O Lord, Thou shalt open my lips, and my mouth shall declare Thy praise.

For if Thou hadst desired sacrifice, I had given it; with whole-burnt offerings Thou shalt not be pleased.

A sacrifice unto God is a broken spirit; a heart that is broken and humbled God will not despise.

Do good, O Lord, in Thy good pleasure unto Sion, and let the walls of Jerusalem be builded.

Then shalt Thou be pleased with a sacrifice of righteousness, with oblation and whole-burnt offerings.

Then shall they offer bullocks upon Thine altar.

The Symbol of the Orthodox Faith

I BELIEVE in one God, the Father Almighty, Maker of heaven and earth, and of all things visible and invisible.

And in one Lord Jesus Christ, the only-begotten Son of God; begotten of the Father before all ages; Light from Light, True God from True God, begotten, not made, of one essence with the Father, through Whom all things were made: Who for us men, and for our salvation, came down from Heaven, and was incarnate by the Holy Spirit and the Virgin Mary, and became Man: And was crucified for us under Pontius Pilate, and suffered and was buried: And He rose on the third day according to the Scriptures: And ascended into Heaven, and sitteth at the right hand of the Father. And shall come again, with glory, to judge both the living and the dead; Whose kingdom shall have no end.

And in the Holy Spirit, the Lord, the Giver of Life; Who proceedeth from the Father; Who with the Father and the Son together is worshipped and glorified; Who spake by the Prophets.

And in One, Holy, Catholic and Apostolic Church. I confess one Baptism for the remission of sins. I look for the Resurrection of the Dead; And the life of the Age to come. AMEN.

First Prayer of St. Macarius the Great

O GOD, cleanse me, a sinner, for I have never done anything good in Thy sight; but deliver me from the evil one, and let Thy will be done in me, that I may open mine unworthy mouth without condemnation, and praise Thy holy name: of the Father, and of the Son, and of the Holy Spirit, both now and ever, and unto the ages of ages. AMEN.

Second Prayer of St. Macarius the Great

HAVING risen from sleep, I offer unto Thee, O Saviour, the midnight hymn, and falling down I cry unto Thee: Grant me not to fall asleep in the death of sin, but have compassion on me, O Thou Who wast voluntarily crucified, and hasten to raise me, who am prostrate in idleness, and save me in prayer and intercession; and after the night's sleep shine upon me a sinless day, O Christ God, and save me.

Third Prayer of St. Macarius the Great

H AVING risen from sleep, I hasten to Thee, O Lord, Lover of mankind, and by Thy loving-kindness, I strive to do Thy work, and I pray to Thee: Help me at all times, in everything, and deliver me from every worldly, evil thing and every attack of the devil, and save me, and lead me into Thine eternal kingdom. For Thou art my Creator, and the Giver and Provider of everything good, and in Thee is all my hope, and unto Thee do I send up glory, both now and ever, and unto the ages of ages. AMEN.

Fourth Prayer of St. Macarius the Great

O LORD, Who in Thine abundant goodness and Thy great compassion hast granted me, Thy servant, to go through the time of the night that is past without attack from any opposing evil: Do Thou Thyself, O Master, Creator of all things, vouchsafe me by Thy true light and with an enlightened heart to do Thy will, both now and ever, and unto the ages of ages. AMEN.

Fifth Prayer of St. Macarius the Great

A LMIGHTY Lord God, Who dost receive from Thy Heavenly Powers the thrice-holy hymn, receive also from me, Thy unworthy servant, this song of the night, and grant me every year of my life and at every hour to send up glory to Thee, Father, Son and Holy Spirit, both now and ever, and unto the ages of ages. AMEN.

First Prayer of St. Basil the Great

A LMIGHTY Lord, God of hosts and of all flesh, Who dwellest on high and lookest down on things that are lowly, Who searchest the heart and innermost being, and clearly foreknowest the secrets of men, O unoriginate and everlasting Light, with Whom there is no variableness, neither shadow of turning:

Do Thou, O Immortal King, receive our supplications which we, daring because of the multitude of Thy compassions, offer Thee at the present time from defiled lips; and forgive us all our sins, in deed, word, and thought, whether committed by us knowingly or in ignorance, and cleanse us from every defilement of flesh and spirit.

Grant us to pass through the night of the whole present life with watchful heart and sober thought, ever expecting the coming of the bright and appointed day of Thine Only-begotten Son, our Lord and God and Saviour, Jesus Christ, whereon the judge of all shall come with glory to reward each according to his deeds.

May we not be found fallen and idle, but watching, and upright in activity, ready to accompany Him into the joy and divine palace of His glory, where there is the ceaseless sound of those that keep festival, and the unspeakable delight of those that behold the ineffable beauty of Thy countenance.

For Thou art the true Light that enlightenest and sanctifiest all, and all creation doth hymn Thee unto the ages of ages. AMEN.

Second Prayer of St. Basil the Great

WE BLESS Thee, O Most High God and Lord of mercy, Who ever doest with us things both great and inscrutable, both glorious and awesome, of which there is no measure; Who grantest to us sleep for rest from our infirmities, and relaxation from the labours of our much toiling flesh.

We thank Thee that Thou hast not destroyed us with our sins, but hast shown Thy loving-kindness to mankind as usual, and while we were lying in despair upon our beds, Thou hast raised us up that we might glorify Thy dominion.

Therefore we implore Thy incomparable goodness, enlighten the eyes of our understanding and raise up our mind from the heavy sleep of indolence; open our mouth and fill it with Thy praise, that we may be able undistracted to sing and confess Thee, Who art God glorified in all and by all, the unoriginate Father, with Thine Only-begotten Son, and Thine All-holy and good and life-giving Spirit, both now and ever, and unto the ages of ages. AMEN.

Midnight Song to the Most Holy Mother of God

I sing of thy grace, O Sovereign Lady, and I pray thee to grace my mind.

Teach me to step aright in the way of Christ's commandments.

Strengthen me to keep awake in song, and drive away the sleep of despondency.

O Bride of God, by thy prayers release me, bound with the bonds of sin.

Guard me by night and by day, and deliver me from foes that defeat me.

O bearer of God the Giver of Life, enliven me who am deadened by passions.

O bearer of the unwaning Light, enlighten my blinded soul.

O marvellous palace of the Master, make me to be a house of the Divine Spirit.

O bearer of the Healer, heal the perennial passions of my soul.

Guide me to the path of repentance, for I am tossed in the storm of life.

Deliver me from eternal fire, and from evil worms, and from Tartarus.

Let me not be exposed to the rejoicing of demons, guilty as I am of many sins.

Renew me, grown old from senseless sins, O most immaculate one.

Present me untouched by all torments, and pray for me to the Master of all.

Vouchsafe me to find the joys of heaven with all the saints.

O most holy Virgin, hearken unto the voice of thine unprofitable servant.

Grant me torrents of tears, O most pure one, to cleanse my soul from impurity.

I offer the groans of my heart to thee unceasingly; strive for me, O Sovereign Lady.

Accept my service of supplication and offer it to compassionate God.

O thou who art above the angels, raise me above this world's confusion.

O Light-bearing heavenly tabernacle, direct the grace of the Spirit in me.

I raise my hands and lips in thy praise, defiled as they are by impurity, O all-immaculate one.

Deliver me from soul-corrupting evils, and fervently intercede to Christ to Whom is due all honour and worship, both now and ever, and unto the ages of ages. AMEN.

Prayer to our Lord Jesus Christ

O MY plenteously-merciful and all-merciful God, Lord Jesus Christ, through Thy great love Thou didst come down and become incarnate so that Thou mightest save all.

And again, O Saviour, save me by Thy grace, I pray Thee. For if Thou shouldst save me for my works, this would not be grace or a gift, but rather a duty; yea, Thou Who art great in compassion and ineffable in mercy.

For he that believeth in Me, Thou hast said, O my Christ, shall live and never see death. If, then, faith in Thee saveth the desperate, behold, I believe, save me, for Thou art my God and Creator.

Let faith instead of works be imputed to me, O my God, for Thou wilt find no works which could justify me. But may my faith suffice instead of all works, may it answer for, may it acquit me, may it make me a partaker of Thine eternal glory.

And may Satan not seize me, O Word, and boast that he hath torn me from Thy hand and fold. O Christ, my Saviour, whether I will or not, save me. Make haste, quick, quick, for I perish.

Thou art my God from my mother's womb. Grant me, O Lord, to love Thee now as once I loved sin, and also to work for Thee without idleness, as I worked before for deceptive Satan.

But supremely shall I work for Thee, my Lord and God, Jesus Christ, all the days of my life, both now and ever, and unto the ages of ages. AMEN.

Prayer to the Guardian Angel of Human Life

O HOLY angel that intercedeth for my wretched soul and my passionate life, forsake not me, a sinner, nor shrink from me because of mine intemperance. Give no place for the cunning demon to master me through the violence of my mortal body, strengthen my poor and feeble hand, and guide me in the way of salvation.

Yea, O holy angel of God, guardian and protector of my wretched soul and body, forgive me all wherein I have offended thee all the days of my life; and if I have sinned during the past night, protect me during the present day, and guard me from every temptation of the enemy, that I may not anger God by any sin.

And pray to the Lord for me, that He may strengthen me in His fear, and show me, His servant, to be worthy of His goodness. AMEN.

Prayer to the Most Holy Mother of God

O MOST holy lady Theotokos, through thy holy and all-powerful prayers, banish from me, thy lowly and wretched servant, despondency, forgetfulness, folly, carelessness, *(some will insert here specific sins and passions which afflict them)* and all filthy, evil, and blasphemous thoughts from my wretched heart and my darkened mind. And quench the flame of my passions, for I am poor and wretched, and deliver me from many and cruel memories and deeds, and free me from all their evil effects. For blessed art thou by all generations, and glorified is thy most honourable name unto the ages of ages. AMEN.

Prayers to the Mother of God

O VIRGIN Mother of God, rejoice, Mary full of grace; the Lord is with thee. Blessed art thou amongst women, and blessed is the fruit of thy womb, for thou hast borne the Saviour of our souls.

Under thy tender compassion we run, O Mother of God, reject not our prayer in our trouble, but deliver us from harm, only pure, only blessed one.

Most glorious Ever-Virgin, Mother of Christ our God, present our prayer to thy Son and our God and pray that through thee He may save our souls.

Prayer for Intercession to the Angelic Hosts

O Heavenly Hosts of holy Angels and Archangels, pray for us sinners.

Prayer for Intercession to all Saints

O glorious Apostles, Prophets and Martyrs, and all Saints, pray for us sinners.

Prayerful Invocation to the Saint Whose Name we bear

Pray for me Saint...*(name)*..., for with fervour I come to thee, speedy helper, and intercessor for my soul.

The Troparion to the Cross

O LORD, save Thy people, and bless Thine inheritance; grant victory to Orthodox Christians over adversaries; and by the power of Thy Cross do Thou preserve Thy commonwealth.

I T IS truly meet to bless thee, O Theotokos, ever-blessed and most-pure and the Mother of our God. More honourable than the Cherubim, and beyond compare more glorious than the Seraphim, without defilement thou gavest birth to God the Word, True Theotokos, we magnify thee.

Glory to the Father, and to the Son, and to the Holy Spirit, both now and ever, and unto the ages of ages. AMEN.

Lord, have mercy. *(Thrice)*

God be gracious to us and bless us, and shine Thy countenance upon us and have mercy upon us.

This is the day which the Lord has made; let us rejoice and be glad in it.

Commemoration of the Living and Departed

R EMEMBER, O Lord Jesus Christ our God, Thy mercies and compassions which are from the ages, for the sake of which Thou didst become man and didst will to endure crucifixion and death for the salvation of those that rightly believe in Thee; and having risen from the dead didst ascend into the heavens and sittest at the right hand of God the Father, and regardest the humble entreaties of those that call upon Thee with all their heart; incline Thine ear, and hearken unto the humble supplication of me, Thine unprofitable servant, as an odour of spiritual fragrance, which I offer unto Thee for all Thy people.

The Church

A ND FIRST, remember Thy Holy, Catholic, and Apostolic Church, which Thou hast provided through Thy precious Blood, and establish, and strengthen, and expand, increase, pacify, and keep Her unconquerable by the power of hell. Calm the dissensions of the Churches, and foil the plans of the powers of darkness, dispel the prejudice of the nations, and quickly ruin and root out the risings of heresy, and frustrate them by the power of the Holy Spirit. *(Bow)*

Save, O Lord, and have mercy on our President/Queen and all in authority throughout the world, commanders-in-chief of armies and navies and air fleets, governors of states/provinces and cities, and all the Christ-loving navies, armies and police; protect their power with peace, and subdue under their feet every enemy and foe, and speak peace and blessing in their hearts for Thy Holy Church, and for all Thy people, and grant that in their calm we too may lead a quiet and peaceful life in true belief, in all piety and honesty. *(Bow)*

Save, O Lord, and have mercy on the holy Eastern Orthodox patriarchs, most reverend metropolitans, Orthodox archbishops and bishops, and all the priestly and monastic order, and all who serve in the Church, whom Thou hast appointed to shepherd Thy rational flock, and through their prayers have mercy and save me, a sinner. *(Bow)*

Save, O Lord, and have mercy on our father *(parish priest or abbot of monastery)*, with all his brethren in Christ, and by their prayers have mercy on me, wretch that I am. *(Bow)*

Save, O Lord, and have mercy on my Spiritual Father ...*(name)*... and by his prayers forgive me my sins. *(Bow)*

Save, O Lord, and have mercy on my parents ...*(names)*..., my brothers and sisters and all my relatives, and the neighbours of my family, and friends and grant them Thy worldly and spiritual goods. *(Bow)*

Save, O Lord, and have mercy according to the multitude of Thy bounties, on all priests, monks and nuns, and on all living in virginity, devotion and fasting, in monasteries, in deserts, in caves, on mountains, on pillars, in hermitages, in the clefts of rocks, and right faith in every place of Thy dominion, and devoutly serving Thee, and praying to Thee. Lighten their burden, console them in their afflictions, and grant them strength, power and perseverance in their struggle, and by their prayers grant me remission of sins. *(Bow)*

Save, O Lord, and have mercy on the old and the young, the poor and destitute, the orphans and widows, and those in sickness and sorrow, misfortune and tribulation, captives and exiles, in prisons and reformatories, and especially on those of Thy servants suffering persecution for Thy sake and for the Orthodox Faith from godless peoples, apostates, and heretics. Visit, strengthen, comfort, and heal them, and by Thy power quickly grant them relief, freedom and deliverance. *(Bow)*

Save, O Lord, and have mercy on those whom I have offended or scandalized by my madness or inadvertence, and whom I have turned from the way of salvation, and whom I have led into evil and harmful deeds. By Thy divine providence restore them again to the way of salvation. *(Bow)*

Save, O Lord, and have mercy on those who hate and offend me, and do me harm, and let them not perish through me, a sinner. *(Bow)*

Illumine with the light of grace all apostates from the Orthodox Faith, and those blinded by pernicious heresies, and draw them to Thyself, and unite them to Thy Holy, Apostolic, Catholic Church. *(Bow)*

For Those Departed in Sleep

REMEMBER, O Lord, those that have departed this life, Orthodox kings and queens, princes and princesses, most holy patriarchs, most reverend metropolitans, Orthodox archbishops and bishops, those in priestly and clerical orders of the Church, and those that have served Thee in the monastic order, and grant them rest with the saints in Thine eternal tabernacles. *(Bow)*

Prayer of Remembrance for Parents Departed in Sleep

REMEMBER, O Lord, the souls of Thy servants who have departed in sleep, my parents *...(names)...,* and all my relatives according to the flesh; forgive them every transgression, voluntary and involuntary; grant them Thy Kingdom and a part in Thy eternal joys, and the delight of Thy blessed and everlasting life. *(Bow)*

All other departed Orthodox Christians

REMEMBER, O Lord, also all our fathers and brethren, and sisters, and those that lie here, and all Orthodox Christians that departed in the hope of resurrection and life eternal, and settle them with Thy saints, where the light of Thy countenance shall visit them, and have mercy on us, for Thou art good and the Lover of mankind. *(Bow)*

At the end, say three times:

Grant, O Lord, remission of all sins to our Fathers, Brothers, and Sisters departed in the faith and hope of resurrection, and grant them memory eternal.

Final Prayer

IT IS truly meet to bless thee, O Theotokos, ever-blessed and most-pure and the Mother of our God. More honourable than the Cherubim, and beyond compare more glorious than the Seraphim, without defilement thou gavest birth to God the Word, True Theotokos, we magnify thee.

Glory to the Father, and to the Son, and to the Holy Spirit, both now and ever, and unto the ages of ages. Amen.

Lord, have mercy. *(Thrice)*

O Lord, bless.

The Dismissal

O LORD Jesus Christ, Son of God, for the sake of the prayers of Thy most pure Mother, our holy and God-bearing fathers and all the saints, have mercy on us. AMEN

Prayers at Meals

Before Breakfast

M OST Holy Trinity, have mercy on us. O Lord, wash away our sins. O Master, pardon our transgressions. O Holy One, visit and heal our infirmities, for Thy Name's sake.

Glory to the Father, and to the Son, and to the Holy Spirit, both now and ever, and unto the ages of ages. AMEN.

Lord, have mercy. *(Thrice)*

Christ God, bless the food and drink of Thy servants, for Thou art holy, always, both now and ever, and unto the ages of ages. Amen.

After Breakfast

I T IS truly meet to bless thee, O Theotokos, ever-blessed and most-pure and the Mother of our God. More honourable than the Cherubim, and beyond compare more glorious than the Seraphim, without defilement thou gavest birth to God the Word, True Theotokos, we magnify thee.

Before the Noon Meal

O UR FATHER, Who art in heaven, hallowed be Thy name. Thy kingdom come, Thy will be done, on earth as it is in heaven. Give us this day our daily bread, and forgive us our debts, as we forgive our debtors; and lead us not into temptation, but deliver us from the evil one.

Glory to the Father, and to the Son, and to the Holy Spirit, both now and ever, and unto the ages of ages. Amen.

Lord, have mercy. *(Thrice)*

Christ God, bless the food and drink of Thy servants, for Thou art holy, always, both now and ever, and unto the ages of ages. AMEN.

After the Noon Meal.

WE THANK Thee, O Christ our God, that Thou hast satisfied us with Thy earthly gifts; deprive us not of Thy heavenly kingdom, but as Thou earnest among Thy disciples, O Saviour, and gavest them peace, come to us and save us.

Lord, have mercy. *(Thrice)*

Glory to the Father, and to the Son, and to the Holy Spirit, both now and ever, and unto the ages of ages. AMEN.

Before the Evening Meal

THE poor shall eat and be satisfied, and those who seek the Lord shall praise Him; their hearts shall live for ever.

Glory to the Father, and to the Son, and to the Holy Spirit, both now and ever, and unto the ages of ages. AMEN.

Lord, have mercy. *(Thrice)*

Christ God, bless the food and drink of Thy servants, for Thou art holy, always, both now and ever, and unto the ages of ages. AMEN.

After the Evening Meal

GLORY to the Father, and to the Son, and to the Holy Spirit, both now and ever, and unto the ages of ages. AMEN.

Lord, have mercy. *(Thrice)*

God is with us by His grace and love for man, always, both now and ever, and the ages of ages. AMEN.

EVENING PRAYERS

The Prayer of St. Ephrem the Syrian

This prayer is read on all days of Holy Great Lent, except on Saturdays and Sundays.

O Lord and Master of my life, a spirit of idleness, despondency, ambition, and idle talking give me not. *(Prostration)*

But rather a spirit of chastity, humble-mindedness, patience, and love bestow upon me, Thy servant. *(Prostration)*

Yea, O Lord King, grant me to see my failings and not condemn my brother; for blessed art Thou unto the ages of ages. AMEN. *(Prostration)*

O God, cleanse me, a sinner. *(12 times, with a reverence each time, and then the entire prayer:)*

O Lord and Master of my life, a spirit of idleness, despondency, ambition, and idle talking give me not. But rather a spirit of chastity, humble-mindedness, patience, and love bestow upon me, Thy servant. Yea, O Lord King, grant me to see my failings and not condemn my brother; for blessed art Thou unto the ages of ages. AMEN. *(Prostration)*

Evening Prayers

Before retiring (or if one prefers, before beginning prayers) go through all the points suggested below in your mind and memory.

Give thanks to Almighty God for granting you during the past day, by His grace, His gifts of life and health.

Examine your conscience by going through each hour of the day, beginning from the time you rose from your bed, and recall to memory: where you went, how you acted and reacted towards all persons and other creatures, and what you talked about. Recall and consider with all care your thoughts, words and deeds from morning till evening.

If you have done any good, do not ascribe it to yourself but to God, Who gives us all the good things, and thank Him. Pray that He may confirm you in this good and enable you to do other good things.

But if you have done anything evil, admit that this comes from yourself and your own weakness, from bad habits or weak will. Repent and pray to the Lover of men that He may forgive you, and promise Him firmly never to do this evil again.

Implore your Creator with tears to grant you a quiet, undisturbed, pure, and sinless night, and to enable you on the coming day to devote yourself wholly to the glory of His Holy Name.

If you find a soft pillow, leave it, and put a stone in its place for Christ's sake. If you sleep in winter, bear it, saying: Some did not sleep at all.

IN the Name of the Father, the Son and the Holy Spirit. AMEN.

Lord Jesus Christ, Son of God, through the prayers of Thy most pure Mother and of our holy and God-bearing fathers and of all the Saints, have mercy on us. AMEN.

Glory to Thee our God, glory to Thee.

O HEAVENLY King, the Comforter, the Spirit of Truth, Who art everywhere present and fillest all things, Treasury of blessings and Giver of Life, come and abide in us, and cleanse us of every impurity, and save our souls, O Good One.

Holy God, Holy Mighty, Holy Immortal, have mercy on us. *(Thrice)*

Glory to the Father, and to the Son, and to the Holy Spirit, both now and ever, and unto the ages of ages. AMEN.

O Most Holy Trinity, have mercy on us.

O Lord, blot out our sins.

O Master, pardon our iniquities.

O Holy One, visit and heal our infirmities, for Thy Name's sake.

Lord, have mercy. *(Thrice)*

Glory to the Father, and to the Son, and to the Holy Spirit, both now and ever, and unto the ages of ages. AMEN.

O UR FATHER, Who art in heaven, hallowed be Thy Name. Thy kingdom come. Thy will be done, on earth as it is in heaven. Give us this day our daily bread. And forgive us our debts as we forgive our debtors. And lead us not into temptation; but deliver us from the evil one.

O come let us worship God our King. *(Bow)*

O come let us worship and fall down before Christ, our King and God. *(Bow)*

O come let us worship and fall down before Christ Himself, our King and God. *(Bow)*

Troparia

HAVE mercy on us, O Lord, have mercy on us. For at a loss for any plea we sinners offer to Thee, our Master, this supplication: have mercy on us.

Glory to the Father, and to the Son, and to the Holy Spirit.

Lord, have mercy on us, for our trust is in Thee. Be not angry with us greatly, neither remember our sins; but look upon us now, in Thy tender compassion, and deliver us from our enemies. For Thou art our God, and we are Thy people; we are all the work of Thy Hands, and we call on Thy Name.

Both now and ever, and unto the ages of ages. AMEN.

The door of compassion open unto us, O blessed Theotokos, for, hoping in thee, let us not perish; through thee may we be delivered from adversities, for thou art the salvation of the Christian race.

Lord, have mercy. *(Twelve times)*

Prayer of St. Macarius the Great
to God the Father

O ETERNAL God and King of all creation, Who hast granted me to arrive at this hour, forgive me the sins that I have committed today in thought, word, and deed, and cleanse, O Lord, my humble soul from all defilement of flesh and spirit. And grant me, O Lord, to pass the sleep of this night in peace, that when I rise from my bed I may please Thy most holy Name all the days of my life, and conquer my flesh and the fleshless foes that war with me. And deliver me, O Lord, from vain and frivolous thoughts, and from evil desires which defile me. For Thine is the kingdom, the power and the glory of the Father, Son, and Holy Spirit, both now and ever, and unto the ages of ages. AMEN.

Prayer of St. Antioch to our
Lord Jesus Christ

O RULER of all, Word of the Father, O Jesus Christ, Thou Who are perfect: For the sake of the plenitude of Thy mercy, never depart from me, but always remain in me, Thy servant. O Jesus, Good Shepherd of Thy sheep, deliver me not over to the sedition of the serpent, and leave me not to the will of Satan, for the seed of corruption is in me. But do Thou, O Lord, Who is worshipped God, holy King, Jesus Christ, guard me as I sleep by the Unwaning Light, Thy Holy Spirit, by Whom Thou didst sanctify Thy disciples. O Lord, grant me, Thine unworthy servant, Thy salvation upon my bed. Enlighten my mind with the light of understanding of Thy Holy Gospel, my soul, with the love of Thy Cross, my heart, with the purity of Thy word; my body, with Thy passionless Passion. Keep my thought in Thy humility, and raise me up at the proper time for Thy glorification. For most glorified art Thou together with Thine unoriginate Father, and the Most Holy Spirit, unto the ages. AMEN.

Prayer of St. Ephrem the Syrian to the Most Holy Spirit

O LORD, Heavenly King, Comforter, Spirit of Truth, have compassion and mercy on me, Thy sinful servant, and pardon my unworthiness, and forgive me all wherein I have sinned against Thee today as a man, and not only as a man, but even worse than a beast, my sins voluntary and involuntary, known and unknown, whether from youth, and from evil suggestion, or whether from brazenness and despondency. If I have sworn by Thy Name or blasphemed it in thought, blamed or reproached anyone, or in my anger have detracted or slandered anyone, or grieved anyone, or if I have got angry about anything, or have told a lie, if I have slept unnecessarily, or if a beggar has come to me and I despised or neglected him, or if I have troubled my brother or quarrelled with him, or if I have condemned anyone, or have boasted, or have been proud, or lost my temper with anyone, or if when standing in prayer my mind has been distracted by the glamour of this world, or if I have had depraved thoughts or have overeaten, or have drunk excessively, or have laughed frivolously, or have thought evil, or have seen the attraction of someone and been wounded by it in my heart, or said indecent things, or made fun of my brother's sin when my own faults are countless, or been neglectful of prayer, or have done some other wrong that I cannot remember - for I have done all this and much more - have mercy, my Lord and Creator, on me, Thy wretched and unworthy servant, and absolve and forgive and deliver me in Thy goodness and love for mankind, so that, lustful, sinful and wretched as I am, I may lie down and sleep and rest in peace. And I shall worship, praise, and glorify Thy most honourable Name, with the Father and His only-begotten Son, both now and ever, and unto the ages of ages. AMEN.

Prayer of St. Macarius the Great

WHAT shall I offer Thee, or what shall I give Thee, O greatly-gifted, immortal King, O compassionate Lord Who lovest mankind? For though I have been slothful in pleasing Thee, and have done nothing good, Thou hast led me to the close of this day that is past, establishing the conversion and salvation of my soul. Be merciful to me, a sinner, bereft of every good deed, raise up my fallen soul which hath become defiled by countless sins, and take away from me every evil thought of this visible life. Forgive my sins, O Only Sinless One, in which I have sinned against Thee this day, known or unknown, in word, and deed, and thought, and in all my senses. Do Thou Thyself protect and guard me from every opposing circumstance, by Thy Divine authority and power and inexpressible love for mankind. Blot out, O God; blot out the multitude of my sins. Be pleased, O Lord, to deliver me from the net of the evil one, and save my passionate soul, and overshadow me with the light of Thy countenance when Thou shalt come in glory; and cause me, uncondemned now, to sleep a dreamless sleep, and keep Thy servant untroubled by thoughts, and drive away from me all Satanic deeds, and enlighten for me the eyes of my heart with understanding, lest I sleep unto death. And send me an angel of peace, a guardian and guide of my soul and body, that he may deliver me from mine enemies, that, rising from my bed, I may offer Thee prayers of thanksgiving. Yea, O Lord, hearken unto me, Thy sinful and wretched servant, in confession and conscience, grant me, when I arise, to be instructed by Thy sayings, and through Thine angels cause demonic despondency to be driven far from me: that I may bless Thy holy name, and glorify and extol the most pure Theotokos Mary, whom Thou hast given to us sinners as a protectress, and accept her who prayeth for us. For I know that she exemplifieth Thy love for mankind and prayeth for us without ceasing. Through her protection, and the sign of the precious Cross, and for the sake of all Thy saints, preserve my wretched soul, O Jesus Christ our God: for holy art Thou, and most glorious forever. AMEN.

Prayer

O LORD, our God, in Thy goodness and love for mankind, forgive me all the sins I have committed today in word, deed or thought. Grant me peaceful and undisturbed sleep. Send Thy Guardian Angel to guard and protect me from all evil. For Thou art the guardian of our souls and bodies, and to Thee we send up glory, to the Father, and to the Son and to the Holy Spirit, both now and ever, and unto the ages of ages. AMEN.

Prayer

O LORD our God, in Whom we believe and Whose name we invoke above every name, grant us, as we go to sleep, relaxation of soul and body, and keep us from all dreams and dark pleasures; stop the onslaught of the passions and quench the burnings that arise in the flesh. Grant us to live chastely in deed and word, that we may obtain a virtuous life, and not fall away from Thy promised blessings; for blessed art Thou forever. AMEN.

Prayer of St. John Chrysostom

(Supplicatory prayers corresponding to 24 hours of the day.)

Day

LORD, deprive me not of Thy heavenly joys. Lord, deliver me from eternal torments. Lord, if I have sinned in mind or thought, in word or deed, forgive me. Lord, deliver me from all ignorance, forgetfulness, cowardice, and stony insensibility. Lord, deliver me from every temptation. Lord, enlighten my heart which evil desires have darkened. Lord, I being human have sinned, but Thou being the generous God; have mercy on me, knowing the sickness of my soul. Lord, send Thy grace to my help, that I may glorify Thy holy Name. Lord Jesus Christ, write me Thy servant in the Book of Life, and grant me a good end. O Lord my God, even though I have done nothing good in Thy sight, yet grant me by Thy grace to make a good start. Lord, sprinkle into my heart the dew of Thy grace. Lord of heaven and earth remember me, Thy sinful servant, shameful and unclean, in Thy Kingdom. AMEN.

Night

O LORD, accept me in penitence. O Lord, leave me not. O Lord, lead me not into temptation. O Lord, grant me good thoughts. O Lord, grant me tears and remembrance of death and compunction. O Lord, grant me the thought of confessing my sins. O Lord, grant me humility, chastity and obedience. O Lord, grant me patience, courage and meekness. O Lord, plant in me the root of all blessings, the fear of Thee in my heart. O Lord, grant me to love Thee with all my mind and soul, and always to do Thy will. O Lord, protect me from certain people, and demons, and passions, and from every other harmful thing. O Lord, Thou knowest that Thou actest as Thou wilt; may Thy will be also in me, a sinner, for blessed art Thou for ever. AMEN.

Prayer to our Lord Jesus Christ

O LORD Jesus Christ, Son of God, for the sake of Thy most honourable Mother, and Thy bodiless angels, Thy Prophet and Forerunner and Baptist, the God-inspired apostles, the radiant and victorious martyrs, the holy and God-bearing fathers, and through the intercessions of all the saints, deliver me from the besetting presence of the demons. Yea, my Lord and Creator, Who desirest not the death of a sinner, but rather that he be converted and live, grant conversion also to me, wretched and unworthy; rescue me from the mouth of the pernicious serpent, who is yawning to devour me and take me down to Hades alive. Yea, my Lord, my Comfort, Who for my miserable sake wast clothed in corruptible flesh, draw me out of misery, and grant comfort to my miserable soul. Implant in my heart to fulfil Thy commandments, and to forsake evil deeds, and to obtain Thy blessings; for in Thee, O Lord, have I hoped, save me.

Prayer of Intercession to the Most Holy Mother of God

O GOOD Mother of the Good King, most pure and blessed Theotokos Mary, do thou pour out the mercy of thy Son and our God upon my passionate soul, and by thine intercessions guide me unto good works, that I may pass the remaining time of my life without blemish, and attain paradise through thee, O Virgin Theotokos, who alone art pure and blessed.

Prayer of Intercession to the holy Guardian Angel

O ANGEL of Christ, my holy Guardian, and Protector of my soul and body, forgive me all my sins of today. Deliver me from all the wiles of the enemy, that I may not anger my God by any sin. Pray for me, sinful and unworthy servant, that thou mayest present me worthy of the kindness and mercy of the All-holy Trinity and the Mother of my Lord Jesus Christ, and of all the Saints. AMEN.

(Here one says a prayer to one's Patron Saint.)

Kontakion to the Theotokos

To THEE, the Champion Leader, we thy servants dedicate a feast of victory and of thanksgiving as ones rescued out of sufferings, O Theotokos; but as thou art one with might which is invincible, from all dangers that can be do thou deliver us, that we may cry to thee: Rejoice, thou Bride Unwedded!

Most glorious, Ever-Virgin, Mother of Christ God, present our prayer to thy Son and our God, that through thee He may save our souls.

All my hope I place in thee, O Mother of God: keep me under thy protection.

O Virgin Theotokos, disdain not me a sinner, needing thy help and thy protection, and have mercy on me, for my soul hath hoped in thee.

My hope is the Father, my refuge is the Son, my protection is the Holy Spirit: O Holy Trinity, glory to Thee.

Hymn to the Most Holy Theotokos

IT IS truly meet to bless thee, O Theotokos, ever-blessed and most-pure and the Mother of our God. More honourable than the Cherubim, and beyond compare more glorious than the Seraphim, without defilement thou gavest birth to God the Word, True Theotokos, we magnify thee.

Glory to the Father, and to the Son, and to the Holy Spirit, both now and ever, and unto the ages of ages. Amen.

Lord, have mercy. *(Thrice)*

O Lord, bless.

O Lord Jesus Christ, Son of God, for the sake of the prayers of Thy most pure Mother, our holy and God-bearing fathers and all the saints, have mercy on us. Amen.

Prayer

(Lacking the opportunity of asking pardon of each person.)

O GOD, absolve, remit, and pardon our voluntary and involuntary sins, in word and deed, known and unknown, by day and by night, in mind and thought; forgive us all, in Thy goodness and love for mankind.

Prayer of Intercession

O LORD, Lover of men, forgive those who hate and wrong us. Do good to those who do good. Grant our brothers and relatives their saving petitions and eternal life. Visit the sick and grant them healing. Guide those at sea. Travel with travellers. Struggle alongside the Orthodox. To those who serve and are kind to us, grant remission of sins. On those who have charged us, unworthy as we are, to pray for them, have mercy according to Thy great mercy. Remember, O Lord, our fathers and brothers who have fallen asleep, and grant them rest where the light of Thy countenance shines. Remember, O Lord, those who bear fruit and do good works in Thy holy churches and grant them their saving petitions and eternal life. Remember also, O Lord, us Thy humble, sinful and unworthy servants, and enlighten our minds with the light of knowledge of Thyself, and guide us in the way of Thy commandments, by the prayers of our immaculate Lady, Mother of God, and Ever-Virgin Mary, and of all Thy Saints, for Thou art blessed unto the ages of ages. AMEN.

Daily Confession of Sins

I CONFESS to Thee, my Lord, God and Creator, to the One glorified and worshipped in Holy Trinity, to the Father, Son and Holy Spirit, all my sins which I have committed all the days of my life, at every hour, in the present and in the past, day and night, in thought, word and deed: by gluttony, drunkenness, secret eating, idle talking, despondency, indolence, contradiction, neglect, aggressiveness, self love, hoarding, stealing, lying, dishonesty, curiosity, jealousy, envy, anger, resentment, and remembering wrongs, hatred, mercenariness, and by all my senses: sight, hearing, smell, taste, touch; and all other sins, spiritual and bodily, through which I have angered Thee, my God and Creator, and caused injustice to my neighbours. Sorrowing for this, but determined to repent, I stand guilty before Thee, my God. Only help me, my Lord and God, I humbly pray Thee with tears. Forgive my past sins by Thy mercy, and absolve me from all I have confessed in Thy presence, for Thou art good and the Lover of men. AMEN.

Prayer of St. John of Damascus.

(To be said pointing at the bed.)

O MASTER, Lover of mankind, is this bed to be my coffin, or wilt Thou enlighten my wretched soul with another day? Behold, the coffin lieth before me; behold, death confronteth me. I fear, O Lord, Thy judgment and the endless torments, yet I cease not to do evil. My Lord God, I continually anger Thee, and Thy most pure Mother, and all the Heavenly Hosts, and my Holy Guardian Angel. I know, O Lord, that I am unworthy of Thy love for mankind, but am worthy of every condemnation and torment. But, O Lord, whether I will it or not, save me. For to save a righteous man is no great thing, and to have mercy on the pure is nothing wonderful, for they are worthy of Thy mercy. But on me, a sinner, show the wonder of Thy mercy; in this reveal Thy love for mankind, lest my wickedness prevail over Thine ineffable goodness and merciful kindness; and order my life as Thou wilt.

(As sleep is the image of death, at night we pray for the departed.)

With the Saints give rest, O Christ, to the souls of Thy servants where there is no pain, no sorrow, no sighing, but life everlasting.

And when about to lie down in bed, say this:

Enlighten mine eyes, O Christ God, lest at any time I sleep unto death, lest at any time mine enemy say: I have prevailed against him.

Glory to the Father, and to the Son, and to the Holy Spirit.

Be my soul's helper, O God, for I pass through the midst of many snares; deliver me out of them and save me, O Good One, for Thou art the Lover of mankind.

Both now and ever, and unto the ages of ages. AMEN.

The most glorious Mother of God, more holy than the holy angels, let us hymn unceasingly with our hearts and mouths, confessing her to be the Theotokos, for truly she gaveth birth to God incarnate for us, and prayeth unceasingly for our souls.

Then kiss thy Cross, and make the sign of the Cross from the head to the foot of the bed, and likewise from side to side, while saying:

The Prayer to the Precious Cross

LET GOD arise and let His enemies be scattered, and let them that hate Him flee from before His face. As smoke vanisheth, so let them vanish; as wax melteth before the fire, so let the demons perish from the presence of them that love God and who sign themselves with the sign of the Cross and say in gladness: Rejoice, most precious and life-giving Cross of the Lord, for Thou drivest away the demons by the power of our Lord Jesus Christ Who was crucified on thee, Who went down to hades and trampled on the power of the devil, and gave us thee, His precious Cross, for the driving away of every adversary. O most precious and life-giving Cross of the Lord, help me together with the holy Lady Virgin Theotokos, and with all the saints, unto the ages of ages. AMEN.

(At the time of sleep, say)

Into Thy hands, O Lord Jesus Christ my God, I commit my spirit. Do Thou bless me, do Thou have mercy on me, and grant me life eternal. AMEN.

AKATHIST TO OUR SWEETEST JESUS CHRIST

Kontakion I

TO THEE, the Champion Leader and Lord, the Vanquisher of hell, I Thy creature and servant offer Thee songs of praise, for Thou hast delivered me from eternal death. But as Thou hast unutterable loving-kindness, free me from every danger, as I cry: Jesus, Son of God, have mercy on me.

Oikos I

CREATOR of Angels and Lord of Hosts! As of old Thou didst open ear and tongue to the deaf and dumb, likewise open now my perplexed mind and tongue to the praise of Thy Most Holy Name, that I may cry to Thee:

Jesus All-Wonderful, Angels' Astonishment!

Jesus All-Powerful, Forefathers' Deliverance!

Jesus All-Sweetest, Patriarchs' Exaltation!

Jesus All-Glorious, Kings' Stronghold!

Jesus All-Beloved, Prophets' Fulfilment!

Jesus All-Marvellous, Martyrs' Strength!

Jesus All-Peaceful, Monks' Joy!

Jesus All-Gracious, Presbyters' Sweetness!

Jesus All-Merciful, Fasters' Abstinence!

Jesus All-Tenderest, Saints' Rejoicing!

Jesus All-Honourable, Virgins' Chastity!

Jesus everlasting, Sinners' Salvation!

Jesus, Son of God, have mercy on me!

Kontakion II

As when seeing the widow weeping bitterly, O Lord, Thou wast moved with pity, and didst raise her son from the dead as he was being carried to burial, likewise have pity on me, O Lover of men, and raise my soul, deadened by sins, as I cry, ALLELUIA!

Oikos II

Seeking to know what passes knowledge, Philip asked: "Lord, show us the Father"; and Thou didst answer him: "Have I been so long with you and yet hast thou not known that I am in the Father and the Father in Me?" Likewise, O Inconceivable One, with fear I cry to Thee:

Jesus, Eternal God!

Jesus, All-Powerful King!

Jesus, Long-suffering Master!

Jesus, All-Merciful Saviour!

Jesus, my gracious Guardian!

Jesus, cleanse my sins!

Jesus, take away my iniquities!

Jesus, pardon my unrighteousness!

Jesus, my Hope, forsake me not!

Jesus, my Helper, reject me not!

Jesus, my Creator, forget me not!

Jesus, my Shepherd, lose me not!

Jesus, Son of God, have mercy on me!

Kontakion III

THOU Who didst endue with power from on high Thy Apostles who tarried in Jerusalem, O Jesus, clothe also me, stripped bare of all good work, with the warmth of Thy Holy Spirit, and grant that with love I may sing to Thee: ALLELUIA!

Oikos III

IN the abundance of Thy mercy, O Jesus, Thou hast called publicans and sinners and infidels. Now despise me not who am like them, but as precious myrrh accept this song:

Jesus, Invincible Power!

Jesus, Infinite Mercy!

Jesus, Radiant Beauty!

Jesus, Unspeakable Love!

Jesus, Son of the Living God!

Jesus, have mercy on me, a sinner!

Jesus, hear me who was conceived in iniquity!

Jesus, cleanse me who was born in sin!

Jesus, teach me who am worthless!

Jesus, enlighten my darkness!

Jesus, purify me who am unclean!

Jesus, restore me, a prodigal!

Jesus, Son of God, have mercy on me!

Kontakion IV

HAVING an interior storm of doubting thoughts, Peter was sinking. But beholding Thee, O Jesus, in the flesh walking on the waters, he confessed Thee to be the true God; and receiving the hand of salvation, he cried: ALLELUIA!

Oikos IV

WHEN the blind man heard Thee, O Lord, passing by on the way, he cried: Jesus, Son of David, have mercy on me! And Thou didst call him and open his eyes. Likewise enlighten the spiritual eyes of my heart with Thy love as I cry to Thee and say:

Jesus, Creator of those on high!

Jesus, Redeemer of those below!

Jesus, Vanquisher of the powers of hell!

Jesus, Adorner of every creature!

Jesus, Comforter of my soul!

Jesus, Enlightener of my mind!

Jesus, Gladness of my heart!

Jesus, Health of my body!

Jesus, my Saviour, save me!

Jesus, my Light, enlighten me!

Jesus, deliver me from all torments!

Jesus, save me despite my unworthiness!

Jesus, Son of God, have mercy on me!

Kontakion V

A S OF old Thou didst redeem us from the curse of the law by Thy Divinely-shed Blood, O Jesus, likewise rescue me from the snares in which the serpent has entangled us through the passions of the flesh, through lustful suggestions and evil despondency, as we cry to Thee: ALLELUIA!

Oikos V

S EEING the Creator in human form and knowing Him to be their Lord, the Hebrew children sought to please Him with branches, crying: Hosanna! But we offer Thee a song, saying:

Jesus, True God!

Jesus, Son of David!

Jesus, Glorious King!

Jesus, Innocent Lamb!

Jesus, Wonderful Shepherd!

Jesus, Guardian of my infancy!

Jesus, Nourisher of my youth!

Jesus, Praise of my old age!

Jesus, my Hope at death!

Jesus, my Life after death!

Jesus, my Comfort at Thy Judgment!

Jesus, my Desire, let me not then be ashamed!

Jesus, Son of God, have mercy on me!

Kontakion VI

I N fulfilment of the words and message of the inspired Prophets, O Jesus, Thou didst appear on earth, and Thou Who art uncontainable didst dwell with men. Thenceforth, being healed through Thy wounds, we learned to sing: ALLELUIA!

Oikos VI

W HEN the light of Thy truth dawned on the world, devilish delusion was driven away; for the idols, O our Saviour, have fallen, unable to endure Thy strength. But we, who have received salvation, cry to Thee:

Jesus, the Truth, dispelling falsehood!

Jesus, the Light above all lights!

Jesus, the King, surpassing all in strength!

Jesus, God, constant in mercy!

Jesus, Bread of Life, fill me who am hungry!

Jesus, Source of Knowledge, refresh me who
   am thirsty!

Jesus, Garment of Gladness, clothe my nakedness!

Jesus, Veil of Joy, cover my unworthiness!

Jesus, Giver to those who ask, give me sorrow for
   my sins!

Jesus, Finder of those who seek, find my soul!

Jesus, Opener to those who knock, open my
   wretched heart!

Jesus, Redeemer of sinners, wash away my sins!

Jesus, Son of God, have mercy on me!

Kontakion VII

DESIRING to unveil the mystery hidden from all ages, Thou wast led as a sheep to the slaughter, O Jesus, and as a lamb before its shearer. But as God Thou didst rise from the dead and didst ascend with glory to Heaven, and along with Thyself Thou didst raise us who cry: ALLELUIA!

Oikos VII

THE Creator has shown us a marvellous Creature, Who took flesh without seed from a Virgin, rose from the tomb without breaking the seal, and entered bodily the Apostles' room when the doors were shut. Therefore, marvelling at this we sing:

Jesus, Uncontainable Word!

Jesus, Inscrutable Intelligence!

Jesus, Incomprehensible Power!

Jesus, Inconceivable Wisdom!

Jesus, Undepictable Deity!

Jesus, Boundless Dominion!

Jesus, Invincible Kingdom!

Jesus, Unending Sovereignty!

Jesus, Supreme Strength!

Jesus, Eternal Power!

Jesus, my Creator, have compassion on me!

Jesus, my Saviour, save me!

Jesus, Son of God, have mercy on me!

Kontakion VIII

SEEING God wondrously incarnate, let us shun the vain world and set our mind on things divine; for God

descended to earth to raise to Heaven us who cry
to Him: ALLELUIA!

Oikos VIII

BEING both below and above, Thou didst never falter,
O Thou immeasurable One, when Thou didst
voluntarily suffer for us, and by Thy death our death didst
put to death, and by Thy Resurrection didst grant life to
those who sing:

Jesus, Sweetness of the heart!

Jesus, Strength of the body!

Jesus, Purity of the soul!

Jesus, Brightness of the mind!

Jesus, Gladness of the conscience!

Jesus, Sure Hope!

Jesus, Memory Eternal!

Jesus, High Praise!

Jesus, my most exalted Glory!

Jesus, my Desire, reject me not!

Jesus, my Shepherd, recover me!

Jesus, my Saviour, save me!

Jesus, Son of God, have mercy on me!

Kontakion IX

THE Angelic Hosts in Heaven glorify unceasingly Thy most holy Name, O Jesus, crying: Holy, Holy, Holy! But we sinners on earth, with our frail voices cry: ALLELUIA!

Oikos IX

WE see most eloquent orators voiceless as fish when they must speak of Thee, O Jesus our Saviour. For it is beyond their power to tell how Thou art both perfect man and immutable God at the same time. But we, marvelling at this Mystery, cry faithfully:

Jesus, Eternal God!

Jesus, King of Kings!

Jesus, Lord of Lords!

Jesus, Judge of the living and the dead!

Jesus, Hope of the hopeless!

Jesus, Comforter of the mournful!

Jesus, Glory of the poor!

Jesus, condemn me not according to my deeds!

Jesus, cleanse me according to Thy mercy!

Jesus, take from me despondency!

Jesus, enlighten the thoughts of my heart!

Jesus, make me ever mindful of death!

Jesus, Son of God, have mercy on me!

Kontakion X

WISHING to save the world, O Sunrise of the East, Thou didst come to the dark Occident of our nature, and didst humble Thyself even to the point of death. Therefore Thy Name is exalted above every name, and from all the tribes of earth and heaven, Thou dost hear: ALLELUIA!

Oikos X

KING Eternal, Comforter, true Christ! Cleanse us from every stain as Thou didst cleanse the Ten Lepers, and heal us as Thou didst heal the greedy soul of Zacchaeus the publican, that we may cry to Thee with compunction and say:

Jesus, Treasurer Incorruptible!

Jesus, Unfailing Wealth!

Jesus, Strong Food!

Jesus, Inexhaustible Drink!

Jesus, Garment of the poor!

Jesus, Defender of widows!

Jesus, Protector of orphans!

Jesus, Helper of toilers!

Jesus, Guide of pilgrims!

Jesus, Pilot of voyagers!

Jesus, Calmer of tempests!

Jesus, raise me who am fallen!

Jesus, Son of God, have mercy on me!

Kontakion XI

TENDEREST songs I, though unworthy, offer to Thee, and like the woman of Canaan, I cry to Thee: O Jesus, have mercy on me! For it is not my daughter, but my flesh violently possessed with passions and burning with fury. So grant healing to me, who cry to Thee: ALLELUIA!

Oikos XI

HAVING previously persecuted Thee Who art the Light that enlightens those who are in the darkness of ignorance, Paul experienced the power of the voice of divine enlightenment, and understood the swiftness of the soul's conversion to God. Likewise, enlighten the dark eye of my soul, as I cry:

Jesus, my All-powerful King!

Jesus, my Almighty God!

Jesus, my Immortal Lord!

Jesus, my most glorious Creator!

Jesus, my most kind Teacher and Guide!

Jesus, my most compassionate Shepherd!

Jesus, my most gracious Master!

Jesus, my most merciful Saviour!

Jesus, enlighten my senses darkened by passions!

Jesus, heal my body scabbed with sins!

Jesus, cleanse my mind from vain thoughts!

Jesus, keep my heart from evil desires!

Jesus, Son of God, have mercy on me!

Kontakion XII

GRANT me Thy grace, O Jesus, Absolver of all debts, and receive me who repent, as Thou didst receive Peter who denied Thee, and call me who am downcast, as of old Thou didst call Paul who persecuted Thee, and hear me crying to Thee: ALLELUIA!

Oikos XII

PRAISING Thy Incarnation, we all glorify Thee and, with Thomas, we believe that Thou art our Lord and God, sitting with the Father and coming to judge the living and the dead. Grant that then I may stand on Thy right hand, who now cry:

Jesus, Eternal King, have mercy on me!

Jesus, sweet-scented Flower, make me fragrant!

Jesus, beloved Warmth, make me warm!

Jesus, Eternal Temple, shelter me!

Jesus, Garment of Light, adorn me!

Jesus, Pearl of great price, beam on me!

Jesus, precious Stone, illumine me!

Jesus, Sun of Righteousness, shine on me!

Jesus, holy Light, make me radiant!

Jesus, deliver me from sickness of soul and body!

Jesus, rescue me from the hands of the adversary!

Jesus, save me from the unquenchable fire and from the other eternal torments!

Jesus, Son of God, have mercy on me!

Kontakion XIII

O MOST sweet and most generous Jesus! Receive this our humble prayer, as Thou didst receive the widow's mite and keep Thy faithful people from all enemies, visible and invisible, from foreign invasion, from disease and hunger, from all tribulations and mortal wounds, and deliver from future torments all who cry to Thee: Alleluia! *(Thrice)*

And again Kontakion 1 and Oikos 1 are read.

Kontakion I

TO THEE, the Champion Leader and Lord, the Vanquisher of hell, I, Thy creature and servant, offer Thee songs of praise, for Thou hast delivered me from eternal death. But as Thou hast unutterable loving-kindness, free me from every danger, as I cry: Jesus, Son of God, have mercy on me!

Oikos I

CREATOR of Angels and Lord of Hosts! As of old Thou didst open ear and tongue to the deaf and dumb, likewise open now my perplexed mind and tongue to the praise of Thy Most Holy Name, that I may cry to Thee:

Jesus All-Wonderful, Angels' Astonishment!

Jesus All-Powerful, Forefathers' Deliverance!

Jesus All-Sweetest, Patriarchs' Exaltation!

Jesus All-Glorious, Kings' Stronghold!

Jesus All-Beloved, Prophets' Fulfilment!

Jesus All-Marvellous, Martyrs' Strength!

Jesus All-Peaceful, Monks' Joy!

Jesus All-Gracious, Presbyters' Sweetness!

Jesus All-Merciful, Fasters' Abstinence!

Jesus All-Tenderest, Saints' Rejoicing!

Jesus All-Honourable, Virgins' Chastity!

Jesus everlasting, Sinners' Salvation!

Jesus, Son of God, have mercy on me!

Prayers to Our Lord Jesus Christ

O ALL-WISE and All-gracious Lord, Our Saviour, Who didst enlighten all the ends of the world by the radiance of Thy Coming, and Who didst call us into Thy Holy Church through the promise of the inheritance of incorruptible and eternal good! Graciously look down on us, Thy worthless servants, and remember not our iniquities, but according to Thy infinite mercies forgive all our sins. For though we transgress Thy holy will, we do not deny Thee, Our God and Saviour. Against Thee alone do we sin, yet Thee alone do we serve, in Thee alone do we believe, to Thee alone do we come, and Thy servants only do we wish to be. Remember the infirmity of our nature and the temptations of the adversary and the worldly enticements and seducements which surround us on all sides, and against which, according to Thy word, we can do nothing without Thy help. Cleanse us and save us! Enlighten our minds that we may firmly believe in Thee, our only Saviour and Redeemer! Inspire our hearts that we may wholly love Thee, our only God and Creator! Direct our steps that we may stumblingly walk in the light of Thy commandments! Yea, our Lord and Creator, show us Thy great and abundant kindness, and make us live all the days of our life in holiness and truth, that at the time of Thy glorious Second Coming, we may be worthy to hear Thy gracious call into Thy Heavenly Kingdom. Grant us, Thy sinful and unprofitable servants, to receive Thy Kingdom, and that in the enjoyment of its ineffable beauty; we may ever glorify Thee, together with Thy Eternal Father and Thy Ever-living Divine Spirit unto the ages of ages. AMEN.

Sweetest Lord Jesus, strong Son of God, Who didst shed Thy precious Blood and die for love of my love, I am ready to die for love of Thy love. Sweetest Jesus, my Life, and my All, I love and adore Thee. Thee only do I wish for my Spouse, as Thou dost wish me for Thy bride. I give myself to Thee. I surrender myself to Thee. O Jesus, Thou Whose heart is ever turned to me, heal my heart, that I may feel the sweetness of Thy love, that I may taste no sweetness but Thee, seek no love but Thee, love no beauty but Thee. I have no desire but to please Thee and to do Thy will. Teach me to repent, and to take up the Cross daily and follow Thee with joy. Teach me to pray with faith and love. Thyself pray in me, that with Thee I may love my enemies and pray for them. Jesus, Thou art life in my death, strength in my weakness, light in my darkness, joy in my sorrow, courage in my faint-heartedness, peace in my agitation, obedience in my prayer, glory in my dishonour, and deliverance from my dishonour. Glory and thanks to Thee Jesus my Saviour and Healer. Amen.

AKATHIST TO OUR MOST HOLY
LADY THE MOTHER OF GOD

Kontakion I

QUEEN of the Heavenly Host, Defender of our souls,
we thy servants offer to thee songs of victory and
thanksgiving, for thou, O Mother of God, hast delivered us
from dangers. But as thou hast invincible power, free us
from conflicts of all kinds that we may cry to thee: Rejoice,
unwedded Bride!

Oikos I

AN Archangel was sent from Heaven to say to the
Mother of God: Rejoice! And seeing Thee, O Lord,
taking bodily form, he was amazed and with his bodiless
voice he stood crying to her such things as these:

Rejoice, thou through whom joy will flash forth!

Rejoice, thou through whom the curse will cease!

Rejoice, revival of fallen Adam!

Rejoice, redemption of the tears of Eve!

Rejoice, height hard to climb for human thoughts!

Rejoice, depth hard to contemplate even for the
eyes of Angels!

Rejoice, thou who art the King's throne! Rejoice, thou
who barest Him Who bears all!

Rejoice, star that causest the Sun to appear!

Rejoice, womb of the divine incarnation!

Rejoice, thou through whom creation becomes new!

Rejoice, thou through whom the Creator becomes
a babe!

Rejoice, unwedded Bride!

Kontakion II

A WARE that she was living in chastity, the holy Virgin said boldly to Gabriel: "Thy strange message is hard for my soul to accept. How is it thou speakest of the birth from a seedless conception?" And she cried: ALLELUIA!

Oikos II

S EEKING to know what passes knowledge, the Virgin cried to the ministering spirit: "Tell me, how can a son be born from a chaste womb?" Then he spoke to her in fear, only crying aloud thus:

Rejoice, initiate of God's ineffable will!

Rejoice, assurance of those who pray in silence!

Rejoice, prelude of Christ's miracles!

Rejoice, crown of His dogmas!

Rejoice, heavenly ladder by which God came down!

Rejoice, bridge that conveys us from earth to heaven!

Rejoice, wonder of angels blazed abroad!

Rejoice, wound of demons bewailed afar!

Rejoice, thou who ineffably gavest birth to the Light!

Rejoice, thou who didst reveal thy secret to none!

Rejoice, thou who surpassest the knowledge of
the wise!

Rejoice, thou who givest light to the minds of
the faithful!

Rejoice, unwedded Bride!

Kontakion III

THE power of the Most High then overshadowed the Virgin for conception, and showed her fruitful womb as a sweet meadow to all who wish to reap salvation, as they sing: ALLELUIA!

Oikos III

PREGNANT with the Divine indwelling, the Virgin ran to Elizabeth, whose unborn babe at once recognized her embrace, rejoiced, and with leaps of joy as songs, cried to the Mother of God:

Rejoice, scion of an undying Shoot!

Rejoice, field of untainted fruit!

Rejoice, thou who labourest for Him Whose labour
is love!

Rejoice, thou who givest birth to the Father of our life!

Rejoice, cornland yielding a rich crop of mercies!

Rejoice, table bearing a wealth of forgiveness!

Rejoice, thou who revivest the garden of delight!

Rejoice, thou who preparest a haven for souls!

Rejoice, acceptable incense of intercession!

Rejoice, purification of the whole world!

Rejoice, favour of God to mortals!

Rejoice, access of mortals to God!

Rejoice, unwedded Bride!

Kontakion IV

SUSTAINING from within a storm of doubtful thoughts, the chaste Joseph was troubled. For knowing thee to have no husband, he suspected a secret union, O Immaculate One. But when he learned that thy conception was of the Holy Spirit, he exclaimed: ALLELUIA!

Oikos IV

THE shepherds heard Angels carolling Christ's incarnate Presence, and running like sheep to their shepherd, they beheld him as an innocent Lamb fed at Mary's breast, and they sang to her and said:

Rejoice, mother of the Lamb and the Shepherd!

Rejoice, fold of spiritual sheep!

Rejoice, defence against invisible enemies!

Rejoice, key to the gates of Paradise!

Rejoice, for the things of Heaven rejoice with
the earth!

Rejoice, for the things of earth join chorus with
the Heavens!

Rejoice, never-silent voice of the Apostles!

Rejoice, invincible courage of the martyrs!

Rejoice, firm support of faith!

Rejoice, radiant blaze of grace!

Rejoice, thou through whom hell was stripped bare!

Rejoice, thou through whom we are clothed with glory!

Rejoice, unwedded Bride!

Kontakion V

HAVING sighted the divinely moving star, the Wise
Men followed its light and held it as a lamp by which
they sought a powerful King. And as they approached the
Unapproachable, they rejoiced and shouted to
Him: ALLELUIA!

Oikos V

THE sons of the Chaldees saw in the hands of the Virgin
Him Who with His hand made man. And knowing
Him to be the Lord although He had taken the form of a
servant, they hastened to worship Him with their gifts and
cried to her who is blessed:

Rejoice, mother of the never-setting Star!

Rejoice, dawn of the mystic Day!

Rejoice, thou who didst extinguish the furnace
of error!

Rejoice, thou who didst enlighten the initiates of
the Trinity!

Rejoice, thou who didst banish from power the
inhuman tyrant!

Rejoice, thou who hast shown us Christ as the Lord
and Lover of men!

Rejoice, thou who redeemest from pagan worship!

Rejoice, thou who dost drag from the mire of works!

Rejoice, thou who hast stopped the worship of fire!

Rejoice, thou who hast quenched the flame of
the passions!

Rejoice, guide of the faithful to chastity!

Rejoice, joy of all generations!

Rejoice, unwedded Bride!

Kontakion VI

TURNED God-bearing heralds, the Wise Men returned
to Babylon. They fulfilled Thy prophecy and to all
preached Thee as the Christ, and they left Herod as a
trifler, who could not sing: ALLELUIA!

Oikos VI

BY shining in Egypt the light of truth, Thou didst dispel the darkness of falsehood, O Saviour. For, unable to endure Thy strength, its idols fell; and those who were freed from their spell cried to the Mother of God:

Rejoice, uplifting of men!

Rejoice, downfall of demons!

Rejoice, thou who hast trampled on the delusion
  of error!

Rejoice, thou who hast exposed the fraud of idols!

Rejoice, sea that has drowned the spiritual Pharaoh!

Rejoice, rock that has refreshed those thirsting for Life!

Rejoice, pillar of fire guiding those in darkness!

Rejoice, shelter of the world broader than a cloud!

Rejoice, sustenance replacing Manna!

Rejoice, minister of holy delight!

Rejoice, land of promise!

Rejoice, thou from whom flows milk and honey!

Rejoice, unwedded Bride!

Kontakion VII

WHEN Simeon was about to depart this life of delusion, Thou wast brought as a Babe to him. But he recognized Thee as also perfect God, and marvelling at Thy ineffable wisdom, he cried: ALLELUIA!

Oikos VII

THE Creator showed us a new creation when He appeared to us who came from Him. For He sprang from an unsown womb and kept it chaste as it was, that seeing the miracle we might sing to her and say:

Rejoice, flower of incorruption!

Rejoice, crown of continence!

Rejoice, flashing symbol of the resurrection!

Rejoice, mirror of the life of the Angels!

Rejoice, tree of glorious fruit by which the faithful
 are nourished!

Rejoice, bush of shady leaves by which many
 are sheltered!

Rejoice, thou who bearest the Guide of those astray!

Rejoice, thou who givest birth to the Redeemer
 of captives!

Rejoice, pleader before the Just Judge!

Rejoice, forgiveness of many sinners.

Rejoice, robe of freedom for the naked!

Rejoice, love that vanquishes all desire!

Rejoice, unwedded Bride!

Kontakion VIII

SEEING the Child Exile, let us be exiles from the world and transport our minds to Heaven. For the Most High God appeared on earth as lowly man, because He wished to draw to the heights those who cry to Him: ALLELUIA!

Oikos VIII

WHOLLY present was the infinite Word among those here below, yet in no way absent from those on high; for this was a divine condescension and not a change of place. And His birth was from a God-possessed Virgin who heard words like these:

Rejoice, container of the uncontainable God!

Rejoice, door of solemn mystery!

Rejoice, doubtful report of unbelievers!

Rejoice, undoubted boast of the faithful!

Rejoice, all-holy chariot of Him Who rides on the Cherubim!

Rejoice, all-glorious temple of Him Who is above the Seraphim!

Rejoice, thou who hast united opposites!

Rejoice, thou who hast joined virginity and motherhood!

Rejoice, thou through whom sin has been absolved!

Rejoice, thou through whom Paradise is opened!

Rejoice, key to the Kingdom of Christ!

Rejoice, hope of eternal blessings!

Rejoice, unwedded Bride!

Kontakion IX

A LL angel-kind was amazed at the great act of Thy incarnation; for they saw the inaccessible God as a man accessible to all, dwelling with us and hearing from all: ALLELUIA!

Oikos IX

W E see most eloquent orators dumb as fish before thee, O Mother of God. For they dare not ask: How canst thou bear a Child and yet remain a Virgin? But we marvel at the mystery, and cry with faith:

Rejoice, receptacle of the Wisdom of God!

Rejoice, treasury of His Providence!

Rejoice, thou who showest philosophers to be fools!

Rejoice, thou who constrainest the learned to silence!

Rejoice, for the clever critics have made fools
    of themselves!

Rejoice, for the writers of myths have died out!

Rejoice, thou who didst break the webs of
    the Athenians!

Rejoice, thou who didst fill the nets of the fishermen!

Rejoice, thou who drawest us from the depths
of ignorance!

Rejoice, thou who enlightenest many with knowledge!

Rejoice, ship of those who wish to be saved!

Rejoice, haven for sailors on the sea of life!

Rejoice, unwedded Bride!

Kontakion X

WISHING to save the world, the Ruler of all came to it spontaneously. And though as God He is our Shepherd, for us He appeared to us as a Man; and having called mankind to salvation by His own Perfect Manhood, as God He hears: ALLELUIA!

Oikos X

THOU art a wall to virgins and to all who run to thee, O Virgin Mother of God. For the Maker of heaven and earth prepared thee, O Immaculate One, and dwelt in thy womb, and taught all to call to thee:

Rejoice, pillar of virginity!

Rejoice, gate of salvation!

Rejoice, founder of spiritual reformation!

Rejoice, leader of divine goodness!

Rejoice, for thou didst regenerate those conceived
in shame!

Rejoice, for thou gavest understanding to those robbed of their senses!

Rejoice, thou who didst foil the corrupter of minds!

Rejoice, thou who gavest birth to the Sower of chastity!

Rejoice, bridechamber of a virgin marriage!

Rejoice, thou who dost wed the faithful to the Lord!

Rejoice, fair mother and nurse of virgins!

Rejoice, betrother of holy souls!

Rejoice, unwedded Bride!

Kontakion XI

EVERY hymn falls short that aspires to embrace the multitude of Thy many mercies. For if we should offer to Thee, O Holy King, songs numberless as the sand, we should still have done nothing worthy of what Thou hast given to us who shout to Thee: ALLELUIA!

Oikos XI

WE see the Holy Virgin as a flaming torch appearing to those in darkness. For having kindled the Immaterial Light, she leads all to divine knowledge; she illumines our minds with radiance and is honoured by our shouting these praises:

Rejoice, ray of the spiritual Sun!

Rejoice, flash of unfading splendour!

Rejoice, lightning that lights up our souls!

Rejoice, thunder that stuns our enemies!

Rejoice, for thou didst cause the refulgent Light
to dawn!

Rejoice, for thou didst cause the ever-flowing river to
gush forth!

Rejoice, living image of the font!

Rejoice, remover of the stain of sin!

Rejoice, laver that washes the conscience clean!

Rejoice, bowl for mixing the wine of joy!

Rejoice, aroma of the fragrance of Christ!

Rejoice, life of mystical festivity!

Rejoice, unwedded Bride!

Kontakion XII

WHEN HE Who forgives all men their past debts
wished to restore us to favour, of His own will He
came to dwell among those who had fallen from His grace;
and having torn up the record of their sins, He hears from
all: ALLELUIA!

Oikos XII

WHILE singing to thy Child, we all praise thee as a
living temple, O Mother of God. For the Lord
Who holds all things in His hand dwelt in thy womb,
and He sanctified and glorified thee, and taught all to cry
to thee:

Rejoice, tabernacle of God the Word!

Rejoice, saint greater than the saints!

Rejoice, ark made golden by the Spirit!

Rejoice, inexhaustible treasury of Life!

Rejoice, precious diadem of pious kings!

Rejoice, adorable boast of devoted priests!

Rejoice, unshaken tower of the Church!

Rejoice, impregnable wall of the Kingdom!

Rejoice, thou through whom we obtain our victories!

Rejoice, thou before whom our foes fall prostrate!

Rejoice, healing of my body!

Rejoice, salvation of my soul!

Rejoice, unwedded Bride!

Kontakion XIII

O ALL-PRAISED Mother who didst bear the Word, holiest of all the Saints, accept this our offering, and deliver us from all offense, and redeem from future torment those who cry in unison to thee: ALLELUIA! *(Thrice)*

And again Oikos 1 and Kontakion 1 are read.

Oikos I

A N Archangel was sent from Heaven to say to the Mother of God: Rejoice! And seeing Thee, O Lord, taking bodily form, he was amazed and with his bodiless voice he stood crying to her such things as these:

Rejoice, thou through whom joy will flash forth!

Rejoice, thou through whom the curse will cease!

Rejoice, revival of fallen Adam!

Rejoice, redemption of the tears of Eve!

Rejoice, height hard to climb for human thoughts!

Rejoice, depth hard to contemplate even for the eyes of Angels!

Rejoice, thou who art the King's throne!

Rejoice, thou who bearest Him Who bears all!

Rejoice, star that causest the Sun to appear!

Rejoice, womb of the divine incarnation!

Rejoice, thou through whom creation becomes new!

Rejoice, thou through whom the Creator becomes a babe!

Rejoice, unwedded Bride!

Kontakion I

QUEEN of the Heavenly Host, Defender of our souls, we thy servants offer to thee songs of victory and thanksgiving, for thou, O Mother of God, hast delivered us from dangers. But as thou hast invincible power, free us from conflicts of all kinds that we may cry to thee: Rejoice, unwedded Bride!

Prayer to our Most Holy Lady the Mother of God

M Y MOST gracious Queen, my hope, Mother of God, shelter of orphans, and intercessor of travellers, strangers and pilgrims, joy of those in sorrow, protectress of the wronged; see my distress, see my affliction! Help me, for I am helpless. Feed me, for I am a stranger and pilgrim. Thou knowest my offence; forgive and resolve it as thou wilt. For I know no other help but thee, no other intercessor, no gracious consoler but thee, O Mother of God, to guard and protect me throughout the ages. AMEN

Canon of Preparation for Holy Communion

O HEAVENLY King, The Comforter, the Spirit of Truth, Who art everywhere present and fillest all things, Treasury of blessings and Giver of life: Come and abide in us, and cleanse us of every impurity, and save our souls, O Good One.

Holy God, Holy Mighty, Holy Immortal, have mercy on us. *(Thrice)*

O Most Holy Trinity, have mercy on us.

O Lord, blot out our sins.

O Master, pardon our iniquities.

O Holy One, visit and heal our infirmities for Thy name's sake.

O UR FATHER, Who art in heaven, hallowed be Thy name. Thy kingdom come, Thy will be done, on earth as it is in heaven. Give us this day our daily bread, and forgive us our debts, as we forgive our debtors; and lead us not into temptation, but deliver us from the evil one.

Lord have mercy. *(12 times)*

O come let us worship God our King. *(Bow)*

O come let us worship and fall down before Christ our King and God. *(Bow)*

O come let us worship and fall down before Christ Himself, our King and God *(Bow)*

PSALM 50

HAVE mercy on me, O God, according to Thy great mercy; and according to the multitude of Thy compassions blot out my transgression. Wash me thoroughly from mine iniquity, and cleanse me from my sin.

For I know mine iniquity, and my sin is ever before me. Against Thee only have I sinned and done this evil before Thee, that Thou mightest be justified in Thy words, and prevail when Thou art judged.

For behold, I was conceived in iniquities, and in sins did my mother bear me. For behold, Thou hast loved truth; the hidden and secret things of Thy wisdom hast Thou made manifest unto me.

Thou shalt sprinkle me with hyssop, and I shall be made clean; Thou shalt wash me, and I shall be made whiter than snow.

Thou shalt make me hear joy and gladness; the bones that have been humbled will rejoice.

Turn Thy face away from my sins, and blot out all mine iniquities.

Create in me a clean heart, O God, and renew a right spirit within me.

Cast me not away from Thy presence, and take not Thy Holy Spirit from me.

Restore unto me the joy of Thy salvation, and with Thy governing Spirit establish me.

I shall teach transgressors Thy ways, and the ungodly shall turn back unto Thee.

Deliver me from blood-guiltiness. O God, Thou God of my salvation; my tongue shall rejoice in Thy righteousness.

O Lord, Thou shalt open my lips, and my mouth shall declare Thy praise.

For if Thou hadst desired sacrifice, I had given it; with whole burnt offerings Thou shalt not be pleased.

A sacrifice unto God is a broken spirit; a heart that is broken and humbled God will not despise.

Do good, O Lord, in Thy good pleasure unto Sion, and let the walls of Jerusalem be builded.

Then shalt Thou be pleased with a sacrifice of righteousness, with oblation and whole burnt offerings.

Then shall they offer bullocks upon Thine altar.

Song I — Tone II

Eirmos:

COME, O you people, let us sing a song to Christ our God, Who divided the sea, and made a way for the nation which He had brought up out of the bondage of Egypt; for He is glorious.

Create in me a clean heart, O God, and renew a right spirit within me.

Troparia:

MAY Thy holy Body be for me the bread of eternal life, O gracious Lord, and may Thy precious Blood be a remedy for my many forms of sickness.

Cast me not away from Thy presence, and take not Thy Holy Spirit from me.

DEFILED by misguided deeds, wretched as I am, I am unworthy, O Christ, to partake of Thy immaculate Body and divine Blood, but make me worthy of them.

Glory to the Father, and to the Son, and to the Holy Spirit, both now and ever, and unto the ages of ages. AMEN.

O blessed Bride of God, O good land which produced the unploughed Corn which saves the world, grant that I may be saved by eating it.

Song III

Eirmos:

B Y establishing me on the rock of faith, Thou hast given me power over my enemies, and my spirit rejoices when I sing: There is none holy as our God, and none good but Thee, O Lord.

Create in me a clean heart, O God, and renew a right spirit within me.

Troparia:

G RANT me, O Christ, teardrops to cleanse the dross from my heart, that, purified and with a good conscience, I may come with fear and faith, O Lord, to the communion of Thy divine gifts.

Cast me not away from Thy presence, and take not Thy Holy Spirit from me.

May Thy immaculate Body and divine Blood be for the forgiveness of my transgressions, for communion with the Holy Spirit and for Eternal Life, O Lover of men, and for estrangement from passions and sorrows.

Glory to the Father, and to the Son, and to the Holy Spirit, both now and ever, and unto the ages of ages. AMEN.

O all-holy Lady, Altar of the Bread of Life, which for mercy's sake came down from on high and gave new life to the world, make even me, who am unworthy, worthy now with fear to eat it and live.

Song IV

Eirmos:

F ROM a Virgin didst Thou come, not as an Ambassador, nor as an Angel, but the very Lord Himself incarnate, and didst save me, the whole man. Therefore I cry to Thee: Glory to Thy power, O Lord!

Create in me a clean heart, O God, and renew a right spirit within me.

Troparia:

O MOST merciful One, Who wast incarnate for us, Thou didst will to be slain as a Sheep for the sins of men; therefore I implore Thee to blot out my offenses.

Cast me not away from Thy presence, and take not Thy Holy Spirit from me.

Heal the wounds of my soul, O Lord, and wholly sanctify me, and make me worthy, O Lord, to partake of Thy divine mystical Supper, wretched as I am.

Glory to the Father, and to the Son, and to the Holy Spirit, both now and ever, and unto the ages of ages. AMEN.

Intercede for me also, O Lady, with Him Who came from thy womb, and keep me, thy slave, pure and blameless that I may be sanctified by obtaining the spiritual pearl.

Song V

Eirmos:

GIVER of light and Sovereign Creator of the worlds, guide us in the light of Thy commandments, for we know no other God than Thee.

Create in me a clean heart, O God, and renew a right spirit within me.

Troparia:

AS Thou didst foretell, O Christ, let it be to Thy wicked servant. Abide in me as Thou didst promise; for lo, I am eating Thy divine Body and drinking Thy Blood.

Cast me not away from Thy presence, and take not Thy Holy Spirit from me.

O Word of God, and God, may the live coal of Thy Body be for the enlightenment of me who am darkened, and may Thy Blood be the cleansing of my sinful soul.

Glory to the Father, and to the Son, and to the Holy Spirit, both now and ever, and unto the ages of ages. AMEN.

O Mary, Mother of God, holy tabernacle of the scent of Heaven, make me by Thy prayers, a chosen vessel, that I may partake of the Sacrament of thy Son.

Song VI

Eirmos:

WHIRLED about in the abyss of sin, I appeal to the unfathomable abyss of Thy compassion: Raise me up from corruption, O God.

Create in me a clean heart, O God, and renew a right spirit within me.

Troparia:

O SAVIOUR, sanctify my mind, soul, heart, and body, and grant me uncondemned, O Lord, to approach the fearful Mysteries.

Cast me not away from Thy presence, and take not Thy Holy Spirit from me.

Grant estrangement from passions, and the assistance of Thy grace, and assurance of life by the communion of Thy Holy Mysteries, O Christ.

Glory to the Father, and to the Son, and to the Holy Spirit, both now and ever, and unto the ages of ages. AMEN.

O Holy Word of God and God, sanctify the whole of me as I now approach Thy divine Mysteries, by the prayers of Thy Holy Mother.

Lord, have mercy. *(Thrice)*

Glory to the Father, and to the Son, and to the Holy Spirit, both now and ever, and unto the ages of ages. AMEN.

Kontakion:

DISDAIN me not to receive now, O Christ, the Bread which is Thy Body and Thy divine Blood, and to partake, O Lord, of Thy most pure and dread Mysteries, wretched as I am, and may it not be to me for judgment, but for eternal and immortal life.

Song VII

Eirmos:

THE wise children did not adore the golden idol, but went themselves into the flame and defied the pagan gods. They prayed in the midst of the flame, and an Angel bedewed them: The prayer of your lips has been heard.

Create in me a clean heart, O God, and renew a right spirit within me.

Troparia:

MAY the communion of Thine immortal Mysteries, the source of all goodness, O Christ, be to me light and life and dispassion and the means of progress and proficiency in divine virtue, O only Good One, that I may glorify Thee.

Cast me not away from Thy presence, and take not Thy Holy Spirit from me.

That I may be redeemed from passions, enemies, wants, and every sorrow, I now draw near with trembling, love and reverence, O Lover of men, to Thy immortal and divine Mysteries, singing to Thee: Blessed art Thou, O God of our fathers.

Glory to the Father, and to the Son, and to the Holy Spirit, both now and ever, and unto the ages of ages. AMEN.

O thou who art full of Divine Grace and gavest birth incomprehensibly to the Saviour Christ, I thy servant, unclean as I am, now beseech thee, O pure one: Cleanse me who now wish to approach the immaculate Mysteries, from all defilement of body and spirit.

Song VIII

Eirmos:

SING of the acts of God Who descended into the fiery furnace with the Hebrew children, and changed the flame into dew, and exalt Him as Lord throughout all ages.

Create in me a clean heart, O God, and renew a right spirit within me.

Troparia:

GRANT me, who am desperate, to be a participant now of Thy heavenly, dread and holy Mysteries, O Christ, and of Thy divine Mystical Supper, O my Saviour and God.

Cast me not away from Thy presence, and take not Thy Holy Spirit from me.

I fly for refuge to Thy compassion, O Good One, and I cry to Thee with fear: Abide in me, O Saviour, and I in Thee as Thou hast said; for lo, confiding in Thy mercy, I eat Thy Body and drink Thy Blood.

Glory to the Father, and to the Son, and to the Holy Spirit, both now and ever, and unto the ages of ages. AMEN.

I tremble, taking fire, lest I should burn as wax and hay. O dread Mystery! O Divine Compassion! How can I who am clay partake of the divine Body and Blood and become incorruptible!

Song IX

Eirmos:

THE Son of the Eternal Father, God and Lord, has appeared to us incarnate of a Virgin, to enlighten those in darkness, and to gather the dispersed; therefore the all-hymned Mother of God we magnify.

Create in me a clean heart, O God, and renew a right spirit within me.

Troparia:

THE LORD is good. O taste and see! For of old He became like us for us, and once offered Himself as a sacrifice to His Father and is perpetually slain, sanctifying communicants.

Cast me not away from Thy presence, and take not Thy Holy Spirit from me.

May I be sanctified in body and soul, O Lord; may I be enlightened and saved; may I become by the communion of the Holy Mysteries Thy dwelling, having Thee with the Father and the Spirit living within me, O most merciful Benefactor.

Glory to the Father, and to the Son, and to the Holy Spirit:

May Thy most precious Body and Blood, my Saviour, be to me as fire and light, consuming the fuel of sin and burning the thorns of my passions, enlightening the whole of me to adore Thy Divinity.

Both now and ever, and unto the ages of ages. AMEN.

God took flesh of thy pure blood. Therefore, all generations sing to thee, O Lady, and throngs of heavenly minds glorify thee. For through thee we have clearly seen Him Who is Lord of all united essentially with mankind.

Preparatory Prayers for Holy Communion

(These psalms and prayers are to be read in the morning before Holy Communion.)

IN the Name of the Father and of the Son, and of the Holy Spirit. AMEN.

Glory to Thee, our God, glory to Thee.

O HEAVENLY King, the Comforter, the Spirit of Truth, Who art everywhere present and fillest all things, Treasury of blessings and Giver of Life, come and abide in us, and cleanse us of every impurity, and save our souls, O Good One.

Holy God, Holy Mighty, Holy Immortal, have mercy on us. *(Thrice)*

Glory to the Father, and to the Son, and to the Holy Spirit, both now and ever, and unto the ages of ages. AMEN.

O Most Holy Trinity, have mercy on us.

O Lord, blot out our sins.

O Master, pardon our iniquities.

O Holy One, visit and heal our infirmities for Thy name's sake.

Lord, have mercy. *(Thrice)*

Glory to the Father, and to the Son, and to the Holy Spirit, both now and ever, and unto the ages of ages. AMEN.

OUR FATHER, Who art in heaven, hallowed be Thy Name. Thy Kingdom come. Thy will be done, on earth as it is in heaven. Give us this day our daily bread. And forgive us our debts as we forgive our debtors. And lead us not into temptation; but deliver us from the evil one.

Lord, have mercy. *(12 times)*

O come let us worship God our King. *(Bow)*

O come let us worship and fall down before Christ our King and God. *(Bow)*

O come let us worship and fall down before Christ Himself, our King and God. *(Bow)*

Then the following Psalms:

Psalm 22

THE LORD is my shepherd, and I shall not want. In a place of green pasture, there hath He made me to dwell; beside the water of rest hath He nurtured me. He hath converted my soul; He hath led me on the paths of righteousness for His name's sake. For though I should walk in the midst of the shadow of death, I will fear no evil, for Thou art with me; Thy rod and Thy staff, they have comforted me. Thou hast prepared a table for me in the presence of them that afflict me. Thou hast anointed my head with oil, and Thy cup which filleth me, how excellent it is! And Thy mercy shall pursue me all the days of my life, and I will dwell in the house of the Lord unto length of days.

Psalm 23

THE earth is the Lord's and all that is in it, the world and all who dwell in it He has set it on the seas, and prepared it on the rivers. Who will ascend the mountain of the Lord, or who will stand in His holy place? He who has clean hands and a pure heart, who has not set his mind on vanity or sworn deceitfully to his neighbour. He will receive a blessing from the Lord, and mercy from God his Saviour. These are the kind who seek the Lord, who seek the face of the God of Jacob. Lift up your gates, you princes, and be lifted up, you eternal doors, and the King of Glory will enter. Who is this King of Glory? The Lord strong and mighty, the Lord mighty in battle. Lift up your gates, you princes, and be lifted up, you eternal doors, and the King of Glory will enter. Who is this King of Glory? The Lord of Hosts, He is the King of Glory.

Psalm 115

I BELIEVED and so I spoke; but I was deeply humiliated. I said in my madness: every man is a liar. What shall I give in return to the Lord for all that He has given me? I will receive the cup of salvation and call on the Name of the Lord. I will pay my vows to the Lord in the presence of all His people. Precious in the sight of the Lord is the death of His Saints.

O Lord, I am Thy slave; I am Thy slave and son of Thy handmaid. Thou hast broken my bonds asunder. I will offer Thee the sacrifice of praise, and will pray in the Name of the Lord. I will pay my vows to the Lord in the presence of all His people, in the courts of the Lord's house, in the midst of thee, O Jerusalem.

Glory to the Father, and to the Son, and to the Holy Spirit, both now and ever, and unto the ages of ages. Amen.

Alleluia, Alleluia, Alleluia. Glory to Thee, O God. *(Thrice)*

Lord, have mercy. *(Thrice)*

And then the following prayers:

OVERLOOK my faults, O Lord Who wast born of a Virgin, and purify my heart, and make it a temple for Thy spotless Body and Blood. Let me not be rejected from Thy presence, O Thou Who hast infinitely great mercy.

Glory to the Father, and to the Son, and to the Holy Spirit.

How can I, who am unworthy, dare to come to the communion of Thy Holy Mysteries? For even if I should dare to approach Thee with those who are worthy, my garment betrays me, for it is not a festal robe, and I shall cause the condemnation of my sinful soul. Cleanse, O Lord, the pollution from my soul, and save me as the Lover of mankind.

Both now and ever, and unto the ages of ages. AMEN.

Great is the multitude of my sins, O Mother of God. To thee, O pure one, I flee and implore salvation. Visit my sick and feeble soul and intercede with thy Son and our God, that He may grant me forgiveness for the terrible things I have done, O thou who alone art blessed.

(On Holy and Great Thursday the following is read)

WHEN Thy glorious Disciples were enlightened at the Supper by the feet-washing, then impious Judas was darkened with the disease of avarice, and he delivered Thee, the Just Judge, to lawless judges. See, O lover of money, this man through money came to hang himself. Flee the insatiable desire which dared to do such things to the Master. O Lord, Who art good towards all, glory to Thee.

Lord, have mercy. *(40 times)*

Prostrations as desired. Then these prayers:

First Prayer of St. Basil the Great

O SOVEREIGN Lord Jesus Christ our God, source of life and immortality, Who art the Author of all creation, visible and invisible, the equally everlasting and co-eternal Son of the eternal Father, Who through the excess of Thy goodness didst in the last days assume our flesh and wast crucified for us, ungrateful and ignorant as we were, and didst cause through Thy own Blood the restoration of our nature which had been marred by sin: O immortal King, accept the repentance even of me a sinner, and incline Thine ear to me and hear my words. For I have sinned, O Lord, I have sinned against heaven and before Thee, and I am not worthy to gaze on the height of Thy glory; for I have provoked Thy goodness by transgressing Thy commandments and not obeying Thy orders. But Thou, O Lord, in Thy forbearance, patience, and great mercy, hast not given me up to be destroyed with my sins, but Thou awaitest my complete conversion. For Thou, O Lover of mankind, hast said through Thy Prophet that Thou desirest not the death of the sinner, but that he should return to Thee and live. For Thou dost not will, O Lord, that the work of Thy hands should be destroyed, neither dost Thou delight in the destruction of men, but Thou desirest that all should be saved and come to a knowledge of the Truth. Therefore, though I am unworthy both of heaven and earth, and even of this transient life, since I have completely succumbed to sin and am a slave to pleasure and have defaced Thy image, yet being Thy work and creation, wretch that I am, even I do not despair of my salvation and dare to draw near to Thy boundless compassion. So receive even me, O Christ, Lover of men, as the harlot, as the thief, as the publican, and as the prodigal; and take from me the heavy burden of my sins, Thou Who takest away the sin of the world, Who healest men's sicknesses, Who callest the weary and heavy-laden to Thyself and givest them rest; for Thou camest not to call the righteous but sinners to repentance. And purify me from all defilement of flesh and spirit. Teach me to achieve perfect holiness in the fear of Thee, that with the clear witness of my conscience I may receive the portion of Thy holy Mysteries and be united with Thy holy Body and Blood, and have Thee dwelling and remaining in me with the Father and Thy Holy Spirit. And, O Lord Jesus Christ, my God, let not the communion of Thy immaculate and life-giving Mysteries be to me for condemnation nor let it make me sick in body or soul through my partaking of them unworthily; but grant me until my last breath to receive without condemnation the portion of Thy holy Mysteries, for communion with the Holy Spirit, as a provision for eternal life, and as an acceptable defence at Thy dread tribunal, so that I too with all Thy elect may become a partaker of Thy pure joys which Thou hast prepared for those who love Thee, O Lord, in whom Thou art glorified throughout the ages. AMEN.

First Prayer of St. John Chrysostom

O LORD my God, I know that I am not worthy or sufficient that Thou shouldest come under the roof of the house of my soul, for all is desolate and fallen, and Thou hast not with me a place fit to lay Thy head. But as from the highest heaven Thou didst humble Thyself for our sake, so now conform Thyself to my humility. And as Thou didst consent to lie in a cave and in a manger of dumb beasts, so also consent to lie in the manger of my unspiritual soul and to enter my defiled body. And as Thou didst not disdain to enter and dine with sinners in the house of Simon the Leper, so consent also to enter the house of my humble soul which is leprous and sinful. And as Thou didst not reject the woman, who was a harlot and a sinner like me, when she approached and touched Thee, so also be compassionate with me, a sinner, as I approach and touch Thee, and let the live coal of Thy most holy Body and precious Blood be for the sanctification and enlightenment and strengthening of my humble soul and body, for a relief from the burden of my many sins, for a protection from all diabolical practices, for a restraint and a check on my evil and wicked way of life, for the mortification of passions, for the keeping of Thy commandments, for an increase of Thy divine grace, and for the advancement of Thy Kingdom. For it is not insolently that I draw near to Thee, O Christ my God, but as taking courage from Thy unspeakable goodness, and that I may not by long abstaining from Thy communion become a prey to the spiritual wolf. Therefore, I pray Thee, O Lord, Who alone art holy, sanctify my soul and body, my mind and heart, my emotions and affections, and wholly renew me. Root the fear of Thee in my members, and make Thy sanctification indelible in me. Be also my helper and defender, guide my life in peace, and make me worthy to stand on Thy right hand with Thy Saints: through the prayers and intercessions of Thy immaculate Mother, of

Thy ministering Angels, of the immaculate Powers and of all the Saints who have ever been pleasing to Thee. AMEN.

Prayer of St. Symeon the Translator

O ONLY pure and sinless Lord, Who through the ineffable compassion of Thy love for mankind didst assume our whole nature through the pure and virgin blood of her who supernaturally conceived Thee by the coming of the Divine Spirit and by the will of the Eternal Father; O Christ Jesus, Wisdom and Peace and Power of God, Who in Thy assumption of our nature didst suffer Thy life-giving and saving Passion - the Cross, the Nails, the Spear, and Death - mortify all the deadly passions of my body. Thou Who in Thy burial didst spoil the dominions of hell, bury with good thoughts my evil schemes and scatter the spirits of wickedness. Thou Who by Thy life-giving Resurrection on the third day didst raise up our fallen first Parent, raise me up who am sunk in sin and suggest to me ways of repentance. Thou Who by Thy glorious Ascension didst deify our nature which Thou hadst assumed and didst honour it by Thy session at the right hand of the Father, make me worthy by partaking of Thy holy Mysteries of a place at Thy right hand among those who are saved. Thou, Who by the descent of the Spirit, the Paraclete, didst make Thy holy Disciples worthy vessels, make me also a recipient of His coming. Thou Who art to come again to judge the World with justice, grant me also to meet Thee on the clouds, my Maker and Creator, with all Thy Saints, that I may unendingly glorify and praise Thee with Thy Eternal Father and Thy all-holy and good and life-giving Spirit, both now and ever, and unto the ages of ages. AMEN.

First Prayer of St. John Damascene

O SOVEREIGN Lord Jesus Christ our God, Who alone hast authority to forgive men their sins, overlook in Thy goodness and love for mankind all my offences whether committed with knowledge or in ignorance, and make me worthy to receive without condemnation Thy divine, glorious, spotless, and life-giving Mysteries, not for punishment, nor for an increase of sins, but for purification and sanctification and as a pledge of the life and kingdom to come, as a protection and help, and for the destruction of enemies, and for the blotting out of my many transgressions. For Thou art a God of mercy and compassion and love for mankind, and to Thee we send up the glory, with the Father and the Holy Spirit, both now and ever, and unto the ages of ages. AMEN.

Second Prayer of St. Basil the Great

I KNOW, O Lord, that I partake of Thy immaculate Body and precious Blood unworthily, and that I am guilty, and eat and drink judgment to myself by not discerning the Body and Blood of Thee my Christ and God. But taking courage from Thy compassion I approach Thee, for Thou hast said: "He who eats My Flesh and drinks My Blood abides in Me and I in him." Therefore have compassion, O Lord, and do not make an example of me, a sinner, but deal with me according to Thy mercy; and let these Holy Mysteries be for my healing and purification and enlightenment and protection and salvation and sanctification of body and soul, for the turning away of every phantasy and all evil practice and diabolical activity working subconsciously in my members, for confidence and love towards Thee, for reformation of life and security, for an increase of virtue and perfection, for fulfilment of the commandments, for communion with the Holy Spirit, as a provision for eternal life, and as an acceptable defence at Thy dread Tribunal, not for judgment or for condemnation.

Prayer of St. Symeon the New Theologian

From sullied lips,

From an abominable heart,

From an unclean tongue,

Out of a polluted soul,

Receive my prayer, O my Christ.

Reject me not,

Nor my words, nor my ways,

Nor even my shamelessness,

But give me courage to say

What I desire, my Christ.

And even more, teach me

What to do and say.

I have sinned more than the harlot

Who, on learning where Thou wast lodging,

Bought myrrh,

And dared to come and anoint

Thy feet, my Christ,

My Lord and my God.

As Thou didst not repulse her

When she drew near from her heart,

Neither, O Word, abominate me,

But grant me Thy feet

To clasp and kiss,

And with a flood of tears

As with most precious myrrh

Dare to anoint them.

Wash me with my tears

And purify me with them, O Word.

Forgive my sins

And grant me pardon.

Thou knowest the multitude of my evil-doings,

Thou knowest also my wounds,

And Thou seest my bruises.

But also Thou knowest my faith,

And Thou beholdest my willingness,

And Thou hearest my sighs.

Nothing escapes Thee, my God,

My Maker, my Redeemer,

Not even a tear-drop,

Nor part of a drop.

Thine eyes know

What I have not achieved,

And in Thy book

Things not yet done

Are written by Thee.

See my depression,

See how great is my trouble,

And all my sins

Take from me, O God of all,

That with a clean heart,

Trembling mind

And contrite spirit

I may partake of Thy pure

And all-holy Mysteries

By which all who eat and drink Thee

With sincerity of heart

Are quickened and deified.

For Thou, my Lord, hast said:

"Whoever eats My Flesh

And drinks My Blood

Abides in Me

And I in Him."

Wholly true is the word

Of my Lord and God.

For whoever partakes of Thy divine

And deifying Gifts

Certainly is not alone,

But is with Thee, my Christ,

Light of the Triune Sun

Which illumines the world.

And that I may not remain alone

Without Thee, the Giver of Life,

My Breath, my Life,

My Joy,

The Salvation of the world,

Therefore I have drawn near to Thee

As Thou seest, with tears

And with a contrite spirit.

Ransom of my offences,

I beseech Thee to receive me,

And that I may partake without condemnation

Of Thy life-giving and perfect Mysteries,

That Thou mayest remain as Thou hast said

With me, thrice-wretched as I am,

Lest the tempter may find me

Without Thy grace

And craftily seize me,

And having deceived me, may seduce me,

From Thy deifying words.

Therefore I fall at Thy feet

And fervently cry to Thee:

As Thou receivedst the Prodigal

And the Harlot who drew near to Thee,

So have compassion and receive me,

The profligate and the prodigal,

As with contrite spirit

I now draw near to Thee.

I know, O Saviour, that no other

Has sinned against Thee as I,

Nor has done the deeds

That I have committed.

But this again I know

That not the greatness of my offences

Nor the multitude of my sins

Surpasses the great patience

Of my God,

And His extreme love for mankind.

But with the oil of compassion

Those who fervently repent

Thou dost purify and enlighten

And makest them children of the light,

Sharers of Thy Divine Nature.

And Thou dost act most generously,

For what is strange to Angels

And to the minds of men

Often Thou tellest to them

As to Thy true friends.

These things make me bold, my Christ,

These things give me wings,

And I take courage from the wealth

Of Thy goodness to us.

And rejoicing and trembling at once,

I who am straw partake of fire,

And, strange wonder!

I am ineffably bedewed,

Like the bush of old

Which burnt without being consumed.

Therefore with thankful mind,

And with thankful heart,

And with thankfulness in all the members

Of my soul and body,

I worship and magnify

And glorify Thee, my God,

For Thou art blessed,

Now and throughout the ages.

Second Prayer of St. John Chrysostom

I AM not worthy, O Lord and Master, that Thou shouldest enter under the roof of my soul; but since Thou in Thy love for mankind dost will to dwell in me, I take courage and approach. Thou commandest: I will open wide the doors which Thou alone didst create, that Thou mayest enter with love as is Thy nature, enter, and enlighten my darkened thought. I believe that Thou wilt do this, for Thou didst not banish the Harlot who approached Thee with tears, nor didst Thou reject the Publican who repented, nor didst Thou drive away the Thief who acknowledged Thy Kingdom, nor didst Thou leave the repentant persecutor (Paul) to himself; but all who had been brought to Thee by repentance Thou didst set in the company of Thy friends, O Thou Who alone art blessed always, now and unto the ages of ages. AMEN.

Third Prayer of St. John Chrysostom

L ORD Jesus Christ my God, remit, forgive, absolve and pardon the sins, offences and transgressions which I, Thy sinful, useless and unworthy servant have committed from my youth, up to the present day and hour, whether with knowledge or in ignorance, whether by words or deeds or intentions or thoughts, and whether by habit or through any of my senses. And through the intercession of her who conceived Thee without seed, the immaculate and ever-virgin Mary Thy Mother, my only sure hope and protection and salvation, make me worthy without condemnation to receive Thy pure, immortal, life-giving and dread Mysteries, for forgiveness of sins and for eternal life, for sanctification and enlightenment and strength and healing and health of soul and body, and for the blotting out and complete destruction of my evil reasonings and intentions and prejudices and nocturnal fantasies of dark evil spirits. For Thine is the kingdom and the power and the glory and the honour and the worship, with the Father and the Holy Spirit, both now and ever, and unto the ages of ages. AMEN.

Second Prayer of St. John Damascene

I STAND before the doors of Thy sanctuary, yet I do not put away my terrible thoughts. But O Christ our God, Who didst justify the Publican, and have mercy on the Canaanite woman, and didst open the gates of Paradise to the Thief, open to me the depths of Thy love for mankind, and as I approach and touch Thee, receive me like the Harlot and the woman with an issue of blood. For the one received healing easily by touching the hem of Thy garment, and the other, by clasping Thy sacred feet, obtained release from her sins. And I, in my pitiableness, dare to receive Thy whole Body. Let me not be burnt, but receive me even as these; enlighten the senses of my soul, and burn the stains of my sins: through the intercessions of her who bore Thee without seed, and of the Heavenly Powers, for Thou art blessed unto the ages of ages. AMEN.

Fourth Prayer of St. John Chrysostom

I BELIEVE, O Lord, and I confess that Thou art truly the Christ, the Son of the Living God, Who came into the world to save sinners, of whom I am the chief. And I believe that this is Thy pure Body and Thy own precious Blood. Therefore, I pray Thee, have mercy on me, and forgive my transgressions, voluntary and involuntary, in word and deed, known and unknown. And grant that I may partake of Thy Holy Mysteries without condemnation, for the remission of sins and for life eternal. AMEN.

Lines of St. Symeon the Translator

Behold I approach for Divine Communion.

O Creator, let me not be burnt by communicating,

For Thou art Fire which burns the unworthy.

But purify me from every stain.

Then this Prayer:

OF THY Mystical Supper, O Son of God, accept me today as a communicant. For I will not speak of Thy Mystery to Thine enemies; I will not give Thee a kiss like Judas; but like the Thief will I confess Thee: "Remember me, O Lord, in Thy Kingdom."

And again these lines:

Tremble, O man, when you see the deifying Blood,

For it is a coal that burns the unworthy.

The Body of God both deifies and nourishes;

It deifies the spirit and wondrously nourishes
the mind.

And these Troparia:

THOU hast ravished me with longing, O Christ, and with Thy divine love Thou hast changed me. But burn up with spiritual fire my sins and make me worthy to be filled with delight in Thee, that I may leap for joy, O gracious Lord, and magnify Thy two comings.

INTO the splendour of Thy Saints how shall I who am unworthy enter? For if I dare to enter the bride-chamber, my vesture betrays me, for it is not a wedding garment, and as a prisoner I shall be cast out by the Angels.

Cleanse my soul from pollution and save me, O Lord, in Thy love for mankind.

SOVEREIGN Lover of men, Lord Jesus my God, let not these Holy Mysteries be to me for judgment through my being unworthy, but for the purification and sanctification of my soul and body, and as a pledge of the life and kingdom to come. For it is good for me to cling to God and to place in the Lord my hope of salvation.

THANKSGIVING AFTER HOLY COMMUNION

Glory to Thee, O God;

Glory to Thee, O God;

Glory to Thee, O God.

Anonymous

I THANK Thee, O Lord my God, that Thou hast not rejected me, a sinner, but hast granted me to be a communicant of Thy holy Mysteries. I thank Thee that Thou hast granted me, unworthy as I am, to partake of Thy pure and heavenly Gifts. But, O Lord, Lover of men, Who didst die for us and rise again and bestow upon us these Thy dread and life-giving Mysteries for the wellbeing and sanctification of our souls and bodies; grant that these may be even to me for the healing of my soul and body, for the averting of everything hostile, for the enlightenment of the eyes of my heart, for the peace of the powers of my soul, for unashamed faith, for sincere love, for the fullness of wisdom, for the keeping of Thy commandments, for an increase of Thy divine grace, and for familiarity with Thy Kingdom; that being kept by Them in Thy holiness I may ever remember Thy grace, and never live for myself but for Thee our Lord and Benefactor. And so when I have passed from existence here in the hope of eternal life, may I attain to everlasting rest, where the song is unceasing of those who keep festival and the joy is boundless of those who behold the ineffable beauty of Thy face. For Thou art the true desire and the unutterable gladness of those who love Thee, O Christ our God, and all creation sings of Thee throughout the ages.

Prayer of St. Basil the Great

LORD Christ our God, King of the ages and Creator of all, I thank Thee for all the blessings Thou hast granted me and for the communion of Thy pure and life-giving Mysteries. I pray Thee, therefore, good Lord and Lover of men, guard me under Thy protection and within the shadow of Thy wings; and grant me with a clear conscience until my last breath worthily to partake of Thy holy Mysteries for forgiveness of sins and for life eternal. For Thou art the Bread of Life, the Source of Holiness, the Giver of all that is good, and unto Thee do we send up the glory, with the Father and the Holy Spirit, both now and ever, and unto the ages of ages. AMEN.

Prayer of St. Symeon the Translator

O Thou Who givest me willingly Thy Flesh for food,

Thou Who art fire, and burnest the unworthy,

Scorch me not, O my Maker,

But rather pass through me for the integration of
    my members,

Into all my joints, my affections, and my heart.

Burn up the thorns of all my sins.

Purify my soul, sanctify my mind;

Strengthen my knees and bones;

Enlighten the simplicity of my five senses.

Nail down the whole of me with Thy fear.

Ever protect, guard, and keep me

From every soul-destroying word and act.

Sanctify, purify, attune, and rule me.

Adorn me, give me understanding, and enlighten me.

Make me the habitation of Thy Spirit alone,

And no longer a habitation of sin,

That as Thy house from the entry of communion

Every evil spirit and passion may flee from me
    like fire.

I offer Thee as intercessors all the sanctified,

The Commanders of the Bodiless Hosts,

Thy Forerunner, the wise Apostles,

And Thy pure and immaculate Mother.

Receive their prayers, my compassionate Christ.

And make Thy slave a child of light.

For Thou alone art our sanctification, O Good One,

And the radiance of our souls,

And to Thee as our Lord and God as is right

We all give glory day and night.

Anonymous

MAY Thy Holy Body, O Lord Jesus Christ our God, be
to me for eternal life, and Thy Precious Blood for
forgiveness of sins. And may this Eucharist be to me for
joy, health, and gladness. And in Thy awful second coming,
make me, a sinner, worthy to stand at the right hand of Thy

glory, through the intercessions of Thy holy and most pure Mother and of all Thy Saints. AMEN.

To the Most Holy Mother of God

ALL-HOLY Lady, Mother of God, the light of my darkened soul, my hope and protection, my refuge and consolation, and my joy, I thank thee that thou hast made me, who am unworthy, worthy to be a communicant of the immaculate Body and precious Blood of thy Son. But do thou who didst bear the true Light enlighten the spiritual eyes of my heart. O thou who didst conceive the Source of Immortality, give life to me who am dead in sin. O thou who art the compassionately loving Mother of the merciful God, have mercy on me and give me compunction and contrition of heart, humility in my thoughts, and the recall of my reasoning powers from their captivity. And grant me till my last breath to receive without condemnation the sanctification of the Holy Mysteries for the healing of soul and body. And give me tears of repentance and confession, and of thanksgiving, that I may praise and glorify thee all the days of my life. For thou art blessed and glorified for ever. AMEN.

Then the Song of Symeon is said:

NOW lettest Thou Thy servant depart in peace, O Lord, according to Thy word. For my eyes have seen Thy salvation which Thou hast prepared in the sight of all peoples, the light of revelation for the Gentiles, and the glory of Thy people Israel.

Holy God, Holy Mighty, Holy Immortal, have mercy on us. *(Thrice)*

Glory to the Father, and to the Son, and to the Holy Spirit, both now and ever, and unto the ages of ages. AMEN.

Most Holy Trinity, have mercy on us.

O Lord, blot out our sins,

O Master, pardon our iniquities.

O Holy One, visit and heal our infirmities, for Thy Name's sake.

Lord, have mercy. *(Thrice)*

Glory to the Father, and to the Son, and to the Holy Spirit, both now and ever, and unto the ages of ages. AMEN.

OUR FATHER, Who art in heaven, hallowed be Thy Name. Thy Kingdom come. Thy will be done, on earth as it is in heaven. Give us this day our daily bread. And forgive us our debts as we forgive our debtors. And lead us not into temptation; but deliver us from the evil one.

Grace like a flame shining forth from thy mouth has illumined the universe, and disclosed to the world treasures of poverty, and shown us the height of humility. And as by thy own words thou teachest us, Father John Chrysostom, so intercede with the Word, Christ our God, to save our souls.

Glory to the Father, and to the Son, and to the Holy Spirit.

THOU hast received divine grace from heaven, and with thy lips dost thou teach all men to adore the one God in three Persons. O John Chrysostom, most blessed Saint, we rightly praise thee; for thou art our teacher, revealing divine things.

Both now and ever, and unto the ages of ages. AMEN.

O UNFAILING Intercessor of Christians, O Constant Mediatress before the Creator, despise not the cry of prayer of us sinners but, of thy goodness, come speedily to the help of us who in faith call upon thee. Hasten to offer swift intercession and prayer for us, O Mother of God, who ever intercedest for those who honour thee.

Lord, have mercy. *(Twelve Times)*

Glory to the Father, and to the Son, and to the Holy Spirit, both now and ever, and unto the ages of ages. AMEN.

More honourable than the Cherubim, and beyond compare more glorious than the Seraphim, without defilement thou gavest birth to God the Word, True Theotokos, we magnify thee.

THE ORDER FOR READING CANONS
AND AKATHISTS WHEN ALONE

*Before commencing any rule of prayer, and at its
completion, the following reverences are made (prostrations
or bows), called
"The Seven Bow Beginning."*

O God, be merciful to me, a sinner. *(Bow)*

O God, cleanse me, a sinner, and have mercy
   on me. *(Bow)*

Having created me, O Lord, have mercy on me. *(Bow)*

I have sinned immeasurably, O Lord,
   forgive me. *(Bow)*

My sovereign, most holy Mother of God, save
   me, a sinner, *(Bow)*

O Angel, my holy Guardian, protect me from
   all evil. *(Bow)*

Holy Apostle (or martyr, or holy father *(Name)* pray to
   God for me. *(Bow)*

Then:

Through the prayers of our holy fathers, O Lord
Jesus Christ, our God, have mercy on us. AMEN.

Glory to Thee, our God, glory to Thee.

O HEAVENLY King, The Comforter, the Spirit of Truth,
Who art everywhere present and fillest all things,

Treasury of blessings and Giver of life: Come and abide in us, and cleanse us of every impurity, and save our souls, O Good One.

Holy God, Holy Mighty, Holy Immortal, have mercy on us. *(Thrice)*

Glory to the Father, and to the Son, and to the Holy Spirit, both now and ever, and unto the ages of ages. AMEN.

O Most Holy Trinity, have mercy on us.

O Lord, blot out our sins.

O Master, pardon our iniquities.

O Holy One, visit and heal our infirmities for Thy name's sake.

Lord, have mercy. *(Thrice)*

Glory to the Father, and to the Son, and to the Holy Spirit, both now and ever, and unto the ages of ages. AMEN.

OUR FATHER, Who art in heaven, hallowed be Thy name. Thy kingdom come, Thy will be done, on earth as it is in heaven. Give us this day our daily bread, and forgive us our debts, as we forgive our debtors; and lead us not into temptation, but deliver us from the evil one.

Lord, have mercy. *(Twelve Times)*

Glory to the Father, and to the Son, and to the Holy Spirit, both now and ever, and unto the ages of ages. AMEN.

O come let us worship God our King. *(Bow)*

O come let us worship and fall down before Christ our King and God. *(Bow)*

O come let us worship and fall down before Christ Himself, our King and God. *(Bow)*

Psalm 50

H AVE mercy on me, O God, according to Thy great mercy; and according to the multitude of Thy compassions blot out my transgression. Wash me thoroughly from mine iniquity, and cleanse me from my sin.

For I know mine iniquity, and my sin is ever before me. Against Thee only have I sinned and done this evil before Thee, that Thou mightest be justified in Thy words, and prevail when Thou art judged.

For behold, I was conceived in iniquities, and in sins did my mother bear me. For behold, Thou hast loved truth; the hidden and secret things of Thy wisdom hast Thou made manifest unto me.

Thou shalt sprinkle me with hyssop, and I shall be made clean; Thou shalt wash me, and I shall be made whiter than snow.

Thou shalt make me hear joy and gladness; the bones that have been humbled will rejoice.

Turn Thy face away from my sins, and blot out all mine iniquities.

Create in me a clean heart, O God, and renew a right spirit within me.

Cast me not away from Thy presence, and take not Thy Holy Spirit from me.

Restore unto me the joy of Thy salvation, and with Thy governing Spirit establish me.

I shall teach transgressors Thy ways, and the ungodly shall turn back unto Thee.

Deliver me from blood-guiltiness. O God, Thou God of my salvation; my tongue shall rejoice in Thy righteousness.

O Lord, Thou shalt open my lips, and my mouth shall declare Thy praise.

For if Thou hadst desired sacrifice, I had given it; with whole-burnt offerings Thou shalt not be pleased.

A sacrifice unto God is a broken spirit; a heart that is broken and humbled God will not despise.

Do good, O Lord, in Thy good pleasure unto Sion, and let the walls of Jerusalem be builded.

Then shalt Thou be pleased with a sacrifice of righteousness, with oblation and whole-burnt offerings.

Then shall they offer bullocks upon Thine altar.

The Symbol of the Orthodox Faith

I BELIEVE in one God, the Father Almighty, Maker of heaven and earth, and of all things visible and invisible.

And in one Lord Jesus Christ, the only-begotten Son of God; begotten of the Father before all ages; Light from Light, True God from True God, begotten, not made, of one essence with the Father, through Whom all things were made: Who for us men, and for our salvation, came down from Heaven, and was incarnate by the Holy Spirit and the Virgin Mary, and became Man: And was crucified for us under Pontius Pilate, and suffered and was buried: And He rose on the third day according to the Scriptures: And ascended into Heaven, and sitteth at the right hand of the Father. And shall come again, with glory, to judge both the living and the dead; Whose kingdom shall have no end.

And in the Holy Spirit, the Lord, the Giver of Life; Who proceedeth from the Father; Who with the Father and the Son together is worshipped and glorified; Who spake by the Prophets.

And in One, Holy, Catholic and Apostolic Church. I confess one Baptism for the remission of sins. I look for the Resurrection of the Dead; And the life of the Age to come. AMEN.

Then the Canons and Akathists are read as follows:

- If one Canon or Akathist is to be read it is read straight through.

- If more than one Canon is to be read, the first Song of the first Canon is read. If the Refrain before the final or last two Troparia is Glory... Now ... , it is replaced by the Refrain of the Canon and "Most

Holy Mother of God, save us" (the latter comes before a Troparion to the Virgin). The first Song of the second Canon is read, beginning with the Refrain (the Eirmos of the first Canon only is read), etc. Glory... and Now... are used only as Refrains before the last two Troparia (or last Troparion) of the final Canon to be read. Then the third Song of the first Canon, beginning with the Eirmos, etc. After the third Song: Lord have mercy (Thrice), Glory... Now... Sedalions. When there is more than one Canon, the Kontakion(s) of the second and any additional ones are read after the Sedalions. Glory... Now... is read before the final verses. Then Songs 4, 5 and 6 are read. After Song 6: Lord, have mercy (Thrice), Glory... Now ... Kontakion of the first Canon. Then Songs 7, 8 and 9 are read.

- If an Akathist is read with the Canon(s), it is included after Song 6. All Kontakions of the Canon(s) are read after Song 3 in this case.

  - After Song 9:

  - It is truly meet to bless thee...

  - Trisagion to Our Father ...

  - Have mercy on us... and the rest of the Prayers Before Sleep.

  - If no other prayers are to be read, the closing is as follows:

  - It is truly meet to bless thee...

  - Prayer(s) following the Canon(s).

  - Trisagion to Our Father...

  - Lord, have mercy. *(Thrice)*

  - Glory... Now...

- o More Honourable than the Cherubim...

- o Through the prayers of our holy fathers, O
  Lord Jesus Christ, our God, have mercy on
  us. AMEN.

*Those who are preparing for Holy Communion are obliged
to read three Canons and one Akathist the evening before.
Usually read are the Canons to the Saviour, the Mother of
God, and the Guardian Angel (in that order), and either an
Akathist to the Saviour or to the Mother of God. Those who
desire to carry out this evening rule of prayer daily receive
great spiritual benefit from doing so.*

THE PRAYER RULE OF
ST. PACHOMIUS

This prayer rule was given to St. Pachomius of Egypt by an Angel, which he then used at each hour of the day and night. It is a prayer rule that especially lends itself to memorization, and as such is one that can be done in situations in which it is impractical for one to pray using a prayer book.

THROUGH the prayers of our holy Fathers, O Lord Jesus Christ our God, have mercy on us.

AMEN. Glory to Thee, our God, glory to Thee.

O HEAVENLY King, The Comforter, the Spirit of Truth, Who art everywhere present and fillest all things, Treasury of blessings and Giver of life: Come and abide in us, and cleanse us of every impurity, and save our souls, O Good One.

Holy God, Holy Mighty, Holy Immortal, have mercy on us. *(Thrice)*

Glory to the Father, and to the Son, and to the Holy Spirit, both now and ever, and unto the unto the ages of ages. AMEN.

O Most Holy Trinity, have mercy on us.

O Lord, blot out our sins.

O Master, pardon our iniquities.

O Holy One, visit and heal our infirmities for Thy name's sake.

Lord have mercy. *(Thrice)*

Glory to the Father and to the Son and to the Holy Spirit, both now and ever, and unto the ages of ages. AMEN.

OUR FATHER, Who art in Heaven, hallowed be Thy Name. Thy Kingdom come, Thy will be done, on earth as it is in Heaven. Give us this day our daily bread, and forgive us our debts, as we forgive our debtors; and lead us not into temptation, but deliver us from the evil one.

LORD, Jesus Christ, Son of God, have mercy on us. AMEN.

Lord, Have mercy. *(Twelve times)*

Glory to the Father, and to the Son, and to the Holy Spirit, both now and ever, and unto the unto the ages of ages. AMEN.

O come, let us worship God our King.

O come, let us worship and fall down before Christ our King and God.

O come, let us worship and fall down before Christ Himself, our King and God.

Psalm 50

HAVE mercy on me, O God, according to Thy great mercy; and according to the multitude of Thy compassions blot out my transgression. Wash me thoroughly from mine iniquity, and cleanse me from my sin.

For I know mine iniquity, and my sin is ever before me. Against Thee only have I sinned and done this evil before Thee, that Thou mightest be justified in Thy words, and prevail when Thou art judged.

For behold, I was conceived in iniquities, and in sins did my mother bear me. For behold, Thou hast loved truth; the hidden and secret things of Thy wisdom hast Thou made manifest unto me.

Thou shalt sprinkle me with hyssop, and I shall be made clean; Thou shalt wash me, and I shall be made whiter than snow.

Thou shalt make me hear joy and gladness; the bones that have been humbled will rejoice.

Turn Thy face away from my sins, and blot out all mine iniquities.

Create in me a clean heart, O God, and renew a right spirit within me.

Cast me not away from Thy presence, and take not Thy Holy Spirit from me.

Restore unto me the joy of Thy salvation, and with Thy governing Spirit establish me.

I shall teach transgressors Thy ways, and the ungodly shall turn back unto Thee.

Deliver me from blood-guiltiness. O God, Thou God of my salvation; my tongue shall rejoice in Thy righteousness.

O Lord, Thou shalt open my lips, and my mouth shall declare Thy praise.

For if Thou hadst desired sacrifice, I had given it; with whole-burnt offerings Thou shalt not be pleased.

A sacrifice unto God is a broken spirit; a heart that is broken and humbled God will not despise.

Do good, O Lord, in Thy good pleasure unto Sion, and let the walls of Jerusalem be builded.

Then shalt Thou be pleased with a sacrifice of righteousness, with oblation and whole-burnt offerings.

Then shall they offer bullocks upon Thine altar.

The Symbol of the Orthodox Faith

I BELIEVE in one God, the Father Almighty, Maker of heaven and earth, and of all things visible and invisible.

And in one Lord Jesus Christ, the only-begotten Son of God; begotten of the Father before all ages; Light from Light, True God from True God, begotten, not made, of one essence with the Father, through Whom all things were made: Who for us men, and for our salvation, came down from Heaven, and was incarnate by the Holy Spirit and the Virgin Mary, and became Man: And was crucified for us under Pontius Pilate, and suffered and was buried: And He rose on the third day according to the Scriptures: And ascended into Heaven, and sitteth at the right hand of the Father. And shall come again, with glory, to judge both the living and the dead; Whose kingdom shall have no end.

And in the Holy Spirit, the Lord, the Giver of Life; Who proceedeth from the Father; Who with the Father and the Son together is worshipped and glorified; Who spake by the Prophets.

And in One, Holy, Catholic and Apostolic Church. I confess one Baptism for the remission of sins. I look for the Resurrection of the Dead; And the life of the Age to come. AMEN.

The Jesus Prayer

LORD, Jesus Christ, Son of God, have mercy on me, a sinner. *(100 Times)*

The Dismissal

I T IS truly meet to bless thee, O Theotokos, ever-blessed and most-pure and the Mother of our God. More honourable than the Cherubim, and beyond compare more glorious than the Seraphim, without defilement thou gavest birth to God the Word, True Theotokos, we magnify thee.

Glory to the Father, and to the Son, and to the Holy Spirit, both now and ever, and unto the ages of ages. AMEN.

Lord, have mercy. *(Thrice)*

O Lord, Bless.

O LORD Jesus Christ, Son of God, for the sake of the prayers of Thy most pure Mother, of our holy and God-bearing fathers, and all the saints, have mercy on us and save us, for Thou art good and the Lover of mankind. AMEN.

THE PRAYER RULE OF
ST. SERAPHIM OF SAROV

St. Seraphim of Sarov taught everyone the following rule of prayer:

"Let any Christian, upon arising from sleep stand before the holy icons, and read the Lord's Prayer "Our Father" thrice, in honour of the Most-holy Trinity, then the hymn to the Theotokos "O Theotokos and Virgin, rejoice..." three times as well, and finally, the Symbol of Our Faith once. Having completed this rule, let each one attend to the tasks to which he was appointed or to which he is called.

"During work at home or while traveling somewhere, let him quietly read "Lord Jesus Christ, Son of God, have mercy on me a sinner." If there are others in his vicinity while he is working, let him silently repeat "Lord have mercy," until supper.

"After supper, upon completing his tasks, let him quietly read "Most Holy Theotokos, save me a sinner," and let him repeat this until falling asleep.

"Going to bed, let any Christian again read the above-mentioned morning rule. Thereafter, let him go to sleep, having protected himself with the sign of the Cross." Fr. Seraphim said "Keeping this rule, it is possible, to reach Christian perfection, for the three prayers indicated are the foundation of Christianity. The first, as the prayer given [to us] by Christ Himself, is the model for all prayers. The second was brought from Heaven by the Archangel to greet the Virgin Mary, the Mother of Our Lord. The Symbol [of our faith] contains in brief all of the salvific dogmas of the Christian Faith."

To those who for whatever reason could not complete this little rule, Venerable St. Seraphim recommended reading it under whatever circumstance: during lessons, while walking, and even in bed. He based this advice on the words of the Scriptures "whosoever should call upon the name of the Lord shall be saved..."

The Lord's Prayer

O UR FATHER, Who art in heaven, hallowed be Thy name. Thy kingdom come, Thy will be done, on earth as it is in heaven. Give us this day our daily bread, and forgive us our debts, as we forgive our debtors; and lead us not into temptation, but deliver us from the evil one.

Hymn to the Most-holy Theotokos

O THEOTOKOS and Virgin, rejoice, Mary full of grace, the Lord is with Thee; blessed art thou among women, and blessed is the Fruit of thy womb, for thou hast borne the Saviour of our souls.

The Symbol of the Orthodox Faith

I BELIEVE in one God, the Father Almighty, Maker of heaven and earth, and of all things visible and invisible.

And in one Lord Jesus Christ, the only-begotten Son of God; begotten of the Father before all ages; Light from Light, True God from True God, begotten, not made, of one essence with the Father, through Whom all things were made: Who for us men, and for our salvation, came down from Heaven, and was incarnate by the Holy Spirit and the Virgin Mary, and became Man: And was crucified for us under Pontius Pilate, and suffered and was buried: And He rose on the third day according to the Scriptures:

And ascended into Heaven, and sitteth at the right hand of the Father. And shall come again, with glory, to judge both the living and the dead; Whose kingdom shall have no end.

And in the Holy Spirit, the Lord, the Giver of Life; Who proceedeth from the Father; Who with the Father and the Son together is worshipped and glorified; Who spake by the Prophets.

And in One, Holy, Catholic and Apostolic Church. I confess one Baptism for the remission of sins. I look for the Resurrection of the Dead; And the life of the Age to come. AMEN.

ACKNOWLEDGEMENTS

I must thank Jennifer Leigh for her invaluable proofreading, design and layout assistance and advice; but most especially for her support.

In addition I would like to thank the staff at Starbucks store 11649; especially Liz, Kim, Tasha, Belen and Courtney. for keeping me well caffeinated as I worked on this project.

May God grant each of you many years!

Made in the USA
Middletown, DE
02 January 2024